The Theory of
Price Uncertainty,
Production, and Profit

T0329550

The Theory of
Price Uncertainty,
Production, and Profit

BY CLEMENT ALLAN TISDELL

PRINCETON, NEW JERSEY
PRINCETON UNIVERSITY PRESS
1968

TO MY PARENTS

Preface

This book presents some of my current thoughts upon the
theory of production under conditions of price uncertainty
and pure competition. My motive for starting this work was to
examine some of the effects of price uncertainty and instability
upon production and profit in the hope of obtaining some
insights into agricultural price policy. As Chapter IX shows,
I have not been completely disappointed in this respect.
However, as the study evolved, factors of more general interest
came to the fore. Consequently, this is not an essay in agricultural price policy but an essay in economic theory, which
attempts to integrate diverse theories of behavior under uncertainty and arrive at meaningful theorems. On the matter of
the production decisions of the firm under pure competition,
it combines new advances in the theory of decision-making
with the traditional results of economic theory. But even here,
I have stubbornly refused to be committed to any decision
criterion as having universal application for conditions of
uncertainty. It will be shown that, even in these circumstances,
many interesting economic theorems can be obtained.

Naturally, a great number of persons have had some
influence on these results. But I should like to record my
appreciation of my teachers at Newcastle University where,
as an undergraduate, I discovered, in a "half-baked" form,
some of the ideas which are developed here. I am especially
grateful to Professor F. H. Gruen, who supervised my doctoral
work at The Australian National University and who gave
up much of his time to clarify my problems. Professor T. W.
Swan also helped with some problems, and Professor J.
Pitchford read the completed manuscript and made some
useful comments on it.

During 1965, I was fortunate enough to be a Visiting Fellow
of Princeton University, and while there to have several discussions with Professor W. J. Baumol, O. Morgenstern, and

other University members. All of these discussions were both exciting and encouraging and finally convinced me to publish these results.

Also, I wish to thank Mrs. Lynne Black for her efficient typing and processing of the whole manuscript, all of which was done in a cheerful fashion. Finally, let me record my great indebtedness to the Australian National University, which made this study possible by first awarding me a doctoral scholarship and by then providing me with additional funds to bring the analysis to fruition.

Canberra, A.C.T.   CLEM TISDELL
November 1966.

Contents

The Theory of
Price Uncertainty,
Production, and Profit

CHAPTER I

Introduction and Outline

"We live only by knowing *something* about the future, while the problems of life, or of conduct at least, arise from the fact that we know so little. This is as true of business as of other spheres of activity. The essence of the situation is action according to *opinion*, of greater or less foundation or value, neither entire ignorance nor complete and perfect information, but partial knowledge. If we are to understand the workings of the economic system we must examine the meaning and significance of uncertainty . . .[1]" (F. H. Knight).

Man's imperfection of knowledge has important consequences for his actions and happiness.[2] Fortunately, its influences are not completely chaotic but exhibit orderly and stable patterns which are discoverable, if not in their entirety then to an important extent, by analytical study, observation, and experimental techniques. Already much is understood about the effects of imperfect knowledge upon economic behavior and about its economic consequences, but the field of its nontrivial influences is not completely explored.

It is the purpose of this study to assemble some of the existing results and to progress beyond them at some points. The discussion deals primarily with some influences of price uncertainty upon the production decisions of the purely competitive firm and, in the light of these, with some effects of price uncertainty upon the level of production, the level of profit,

[1] F. H. Knight, *Risk, Uncertainty and Profit*, Houghton Mifflin Company, New York, 1922, p. 199.
[2] Cf. J. Dewey, *The Quest for Certainty*, G. P. Putnam's Sons, New York, 1960, p. 137.

and the choice of "techniques." Although theories of rational behavior play an important role in the analysis, they do not dominate it, for most of its theorems hold under a wide range of behavioral conditions. The analysis would be of much lesser generality if this were not so.

Although some connections are left unstated, the economic theories and problems of the analysis are not treated in isolation but are related to more general theories. Theories of economic behavior are regarded as special cases of more general theories of behavior. This approach, which has been increasingly adopted since the introduction of the theory of games,[3] has proved to be extremely fruitful. Its further possibilities for development seem to be immense.

However, it must be emphasized that the existence of these general abstract theories of behavior does not eliminate the need for particular theories of economic behavior. Yet their use enables us to compare, evaluate, and unify apparently diverse types of behavior in terms of common characteristics. They act to prevent extreme compartmentalization and enable us to draw upon and relate experiences which otherwise might seem unconnected. These general theories ensure substantial economies of thought—they yield theorems of wide scope, theorems which apply not only to much seemingly diverse economic behavior but also to non-economic behavior.

Increased generality is also achieved by exploiting the mathematically similar properties of different behavioral conditions. For example, for the conditions specified in the analysis, the firm's production choice, no matter what the motivation behind it, can be envisaged and treated as resulting from its maximization of an identifiable imputed linear profit function subject to its set of production possibilities. The use of this property leads to a great increase in the generality of the argument.

[3] Von Neumann and Morgenstern, in postulating formal general abstract theories of behavior and in then treating economic and other categories of behavior as special cases, have considerably widened our vision of the social universe. See J. von Neumann and O. Morgenstern, *Theory of Games and Economic Behavior*, Princeton University Press, Princeton, 1st edn., 1944; 3rd edn., 1953.

Since conditions of price uncertainty are central to this study, usage of the term "uncertainty" needs to be clarified. Writers such as F. H. Knight have drawn a distinction between risk and uncertainty. They describe a situation as a risky one if outcomes can be assigned calculable objective probabilities which satisfy the orthodox probability axioms. A situation is described as uncertain if no such probabilities can be assigned.[4] The term "uncertainty" will be used here in a broader sense. A variable will be taken to be of uncertain value for some period if the value which occurs for that period cannot be predicted with zero probability of error.[5] Hence, in this analysis, conditions of price uncertainty involve all those circumstances in which there is some probability that predicted prices and realized prices do not coincide.

Errors of prediction may arise from several sources. Assume that the variable whose value is to be predicted is a particular dependent function of n other independent variables. An error in prediction may occur if the predicting individual relies upon a different function. Again, error may occur not because the functional form of the relationship is incorrect, but because the values of the independent variables are not perfectly known. Furthermore, divergencies may occur because the variable which is to be estimated depends upon a random natural process. This last case allows for the possibility that non-deterministic (random) elements may occur in nature (in reality).[6]

[4] F. H. Knight, *op. cit.*

[5] The probablity of this error may be subjective or objective. It is possible that one type of probability may be positive and the other not. Yet, empirically, it possibly tends to be the case that when one is positive so is the other. Distinctions between and meanings of objective and subjective probabilities will be discussed in Chapter II.

[6] This non-determinism does not necessarily involve chaos, since the indeterminate elements may exhibit regular properties when considered as a collection or group. It is not always possible to decide whether the indeterminacy arises due to limitations of observation or whether in reality a random process is present. In this respect, one might consider the quantum principle of indeterminancy. This principle is discussed, for example, by J. Passmore, *One Hundred Years of Philosophy*, G. Duckworth, London, 1957, pp. 332–333.

There seem to be two important ways in which economic theory needs to deal with the probability of error. First, the predictions of economic theories may not perfectly coincide with observation, and this gives rise to problems of specifying imprecision and of choosing an optimal imprecise theory. Where there are a number of alternative theories of the same phenomenon, each of which gives different patterns of prediction and involves different costs of application, the choice of an optimal theory may become a problem. No single theory may be optimal for all purposes—for some purposes, simpler, less costly, and more erroneous theory may be optimal, and sometimes stochastic models may be optimal. Secondly, economic agents may act under conditions of uncertainty, and the ramifications of this need to be integrated into economic theory. This work directs attention to the second of these matters. Specifically, it deals with implications for production and profit of the behavior of purely competitive firms operating under price uncertainty.

The production models employed in the body of this discussion abstract from the existence of inventories. This course has been adopted in the belief that the introduction of inventories substantially complicates the analysis without changing the general tenor of the results. However, some of the implications of introducing inventories will be considered in an appendix to the analysis.

Now, let us outline the proposed development of the discussion. As previously suggested, theories of the firm's production behavior under price uncertainty can be regarded as special cases of more general abstract theories of behavior and theories of the firm's production decisions can be regarded as special cases of general abstract theories of decision-making. Significant advantage is therefore obtained by considering the general theories at the outset, and this will be done in Chapter II.

Some of the difficulties of devising and defining theories of rational behavior are discussed in Chapter II. Then a theory of rational behavior is suggested which is applicable to uncertainty. This raises the problem of what is meant by "probable" and "possible" and leads us to consider the role of probability weights in decision-making under uncertainty. It is found that probability weights have been given a number of different interpretations and have been assumed to obey a number of different laws. There seems no reason to expect probability weights always to obey the same laws in practice or to refer always to the same type of phenomenon.

The conditions are stated under which different criteria will lead to behavior which is consistent with the theory of rational behavior. The properties of a large group of criteria, some of which rely upon probability weights and some which do not, are examined. They lead us to the conclusion that a great variety of criteria are consistent with rational behavior. Even if behavior is rational, it can be extremely diverse.

Simon's objections to "orthodox" decision theory, in which he includes criteria such as the minimax and the Bayesian, are outlined. He claims that "orthodox" decision theories involve "unbounded" rationality, but it is shown that "unbounded" rationality is not required for rational behavior and that these theories can be reinterpreted so as to accord with bounded rationality.

Then a theory of consistent but not necessarily rational behavior is outlined. This theory includes the theory of rational behavior as a special case, but despite its increased generality, it does not encompass all varieties of possible behavior. With this in mind, it will be our later aim to free the theory from the assumption of particular forms of behavior, i.e. from the assumption of rational or consistent behavior. Throughout the analysis, the decision-making unit is treated as if it is an individual, and, in consequence, some interesting problems of group behavior are ignored. But the direction of the research seems correct in this respect, since the behavior of purely competitive firms is our prime interest.

The theory of consistent behavior is applied in Chapter III to specify the firm's production choices under price uncertainty and to consider the effects upon the firm's "equilibrium" level of production of such criteria as the Wald, the maximax, the Hurwicz, and the Bayesian. Several decision theories, which are abstractly outlined in Chapter II, are applied in Chapter III to determine the firm's optimal production combinations under conditions of price uncertainty.

A proposition is introduced in Chapter III which plays an important role in this analysis. It liberates the analysis from the constraints of particular theories of behavior. It integrates diverse types of production behavior into a coherent general framework. This proposition, which might be called the "maximum equivalence proposition," asserts that, for the production conditions which are stated, any chosen production combination of the firm can be obtained by maximizing an appropriate imputed linear function subject to the firm's production possibility set. The coefficients of the commodity quantities in this linear profit function can be regarded as imputed prices. When the appropriate imputed prices are assigned, maximizing the imputed profit function subject to the firm's production possibility set yields solution values which are equivalent to the firm's actual production combination. The imputed price values of the maximum equivalent problem will in future be referred to as *shadow prices*.[7]

At first, the significance of the maximum equivalence proposition may not be evident. But it has a number of useful consequences. Under certain conditions, the shadow prices which correspond to some decision criteria are easily and generally identifiable, and it may be simpler or less costly to solve the equivalent maximization problem rather than the decision problem in its original form. Again, the proposition implies that the results of standard maximization theorems are relevant, and this will prove to be useful in comparing the influence upon production of various modes of behavior under price uncertainty. Moreover, it enables us, without committing

---

[7] Even though the term "shadow prices" has been used in other contexts, including that of linear programming, its use above should not be confusing.

ourselves to a very particular theory of behavior, to derive general theorems about the influence of price uncertainty and instability upon the firm's level of average profit. "Average profit" is used in this context to indicate the level to which profit tends when it is averaged over a large number of time periods. Furthermore, the use of shadow prices proves to be a boon when considering aggregate production under conditions of price uncertainty, since within a large group considerable variation in behavior and price anticipations is liable to occur. Conversion to this type of extremum problem also brings notational advantages.

The purely competitive firm's shadow prices for criteria such as the Wald, the maximax, the Hurwicz, and the expected gain maximization are derived in Chapter III, and the corresponding maximum equivalent production problems are solved. The maximum equivalence property proves to be especially helpful in Chapter IV when the comparative effects upon the firm's production of different decision criteria, price images, and behavioral patterns are discussed. If suitable differentiability conditions are satisfied, the Hicksian production theorems[8] for the perfectly competitive firm can be employed in this comparison. So, indirectly, existing theorems about the perfectly competitive firm become relevant to the discussion of production behavior under conditions of price uncertainty.

Upon this matter, however, a word of caution is called for. Since static decision-making assumptions underlie a large part of the analysis, it may at first seem that the correspondence between production theorems for price certainty and those for price uncertainty is always straightforward. However, it is clear from Hart's work[9] that no straightforward correspondence is ensured under dynamic decision-making assumptions.

[8] J. R. Hicks, *Value and Capital*, 2nd edn., The Clarendon Press, Oxford, 1946.

[9] A. G. Hart, "Risk, Uncertainty and the Unprofitability of Compounding Probabilities", pp. 110–118 in *Studies in Mathematical Economics and Econometrics*, O. Lange, F. McIntyre, and F. Yntema, eds., The University of Chicago Press, Chicago, 1942.

Although, as Theil[10] has shown, a relatively simple form of certainty equivalence may arise in the dynamic decision-making case if the objective function is quadratic in the controlled variables. The following static decision-making assumption is employed in most of this work: The firm's production combination for any period is "planned" in advance, there is no divergence of its production away from this plan, and its planned output for any period is independent of both its actual and planned output of any other period. The static decision-making assumption is relaxed in Chapter VII, and the firm is permitted to diverge from plan at an additional cost. These naive decision-making assumptions will provide us with some useful insights into the influences of even more complicated decision processes.

So far we shall be chiefly preoccupied with the production decisions of purely competitive firms which are assumed to operate under price uncertainty. But in Chapter V the centre of attention changes. The study of the effects of price uncertainty upon the firm's level of average profit is now the main purpose. Measures of price uncertainty and price instability are defined which enable us, if certain production conditions are satisfied, to isolate the separate effects of these factors upon the level of the firm's average profit. Theorems about the influence of price uncertainty and price instability which are of considerable generality are suggested. Several existing theories are shown to be special cases[11] of the general theory which is developed.

It is a short step from the results of Chapter V to those of the next chapter. In Chapter V the influences of price uncertainty and instability on average profit are considered assuming a *given* production technique. In Chapter VI, using these

[10] H. Theil, *Economic Forecasts and Policy*, 2nd revised ed., North-Holland Publishing Company, 1961, p. 417. For early statements of certainty equivalence see H. A. Simon, "Dynamic Programming under Uncertainty with a Quadratic Criterion Function," *Econometrica*, vol. 24 (1956), pp. 74–81; H. Theil, "A Note on Certainty Equivalence in Dynamic Planning," *Econometrica*, vol. 25 (1957), pp. 346–349.
[11] These include the theories of W. Oi and R. R. Nelson.

results, we can compare the average profit for *alternative* techniques and find out how the average profit from these alternative techniques varies as price uncertainty and instability change. We shall endeavor to discover how the flexibility of a technique affects its likelihood of being adopted as price uncertainty and instability vary. From a knowledge of some general properties of the cost functions, it will be possible to gauge the influence of price uncertainty and instability upon the "excess" average profit of a technique and, consequently, upon its likelihood of adoption. The theory of technique choice is developed in general terms, and the special and erroneous nature of some existing theories[12] is made clear.

However, the static decision-making assumption still underlies our theorems. It is a fruitful assumption, but in many circumstances it cannot be regarded as being better than a rough first approximation. Therefore it is relaxed in Chapter VII. The firm is permitted to diverge from plan, but at a cost, and the previous theorems about average profit and technique choice are extended to take account of this circumstance. The extended theory enables us to assess more generally some of the implications of price uncertainty and to discern some of the behavioral consequences of learning. The theory accommodates the view of Hart[13] and others that increased price uncertainty increases the likelihood of adoption of flexible techniques, but it is made clear that flexibility must be defined in a particular way for this result. This is important since, as indicated in Chapter VI, some erroneous views upon this subject exist. Chapter V–VII also give a more general picture of the influence of price instability upon average profit and technique choice than the existing one, since greater allowance is made for possible "errors." The analysis of these chapters shows that for some error patterns increased price instability increases average profit, but not for others.

All our attention has so far been concentrated on the firm.

[12] This group of theories include those of R. R. Nelson and T. Marschak and of W. J. Baumol.
[13] A. G. Hart, *op. cit.*

But now an attempt is made to consider the wider relevance of price uncertainty. In Chapter VIII some of its possible effects on the level of industry profit are noted. In Chapter IX its effect upon the level of aggregate production is considered.

It is shown in Chapter IX that, under very general production conditions, price uncertainty reduces the aggregate output of the economy below its "maximum attainable frontier." It is then suggested that a variety of forward price schemes can, by reducing the price uncertainty of firms, raise an economy's level of production and consumption. This the forward price schemes may do even if they fall far short of being Pareto optimal. This chapter integrates our previous production results for the firm into a "general equilibrium" context. Finally, Chapter X sums up our results and indicates some further possible developments.

Much of the argument relies upon the properties of convex functions and sets. Merely from a knowledge of the convexity properties of appropriate functions, it is possible to assert a number of general theorems about the effects of price uncertainty and instability on production and profit. But in order to give more detailed theorems it is necessary to define the form of the functions more exactly. For example, a polynomial function has the useful property that the expected value of its dependent variable can be expressed as a linear function of the moments of the independent variables,[14] and under some circumstances it yields a good approximation to more complicated functions.[15] Quadratic functions will be extensively employed in the analysis to obtain comparatively concise theorems about the effects of price uncertainty and instability on profit and production. The quadratic function

---

[14] This result is based on standard statistical theorems of the properties of moments. See, R. Radner, "Mathematical Specification of Goals for Decision Problems", Ch. 11, in *Human Judgments and Optimality*, M. W. Shelly and G. Bryan, ed., John Wiley, New York, 1964.

[15] Taylor's series can be used under a number of circumstances to give a "close" polynomial approximation to a differentiable function. For further details see R. G. D. Allen, *Mathematical Analysis for Economists*, London, 1960, pp. 450–459.

is of particular interest since the average value of its dependent variable is a linear function of the mean, variance, and covariance of its independent variables. For example, if profit can be expressed as a quadratic function of the price of a product, then average profit is a linear function of the expected value and variance of the product's price.

The main aim of the book is to outline some of the regular effects which price uncertainty has upon production and profit and, in so doing, to indicate the benefits which flow from relating economic theories, especially theories of economic behavior, to more general and abstract theories.

CHAPTER II

Some Theories of Decision-Making

A. Introduction and Discussion
of Rational Behavior

The purpose of this chapter is to consider a limited number of theories of decision-making and human behavior. The theories under consideration will be sufficiently general to cover behavior under uncertainty, for behavior under these conditions is our main concern. A study of these abstract theories will enable us to appreciate their applicability to production decisions under price uncertainty.

Economists have often asserted that behavior is, or tends to be rational, but, as Bertrand Russell suggests, "it is difficult to know what one means by it [rational behavior], or whether, if that were known, it is something which human beings can achieve".[1] Also, as R. D. Luce and H. Raiffa point out, "the term 'rational' is far from precise, and it certainly means different things in different theories that have been developed."[2] Boulding warns of the danger that very formal theories of rational behavior "can easily collapse to the empty proposition that people do what they do".[3] There can be little doubt that the term "rational behavior" has been loosely and variously used and that there are major difficulties in constructing a meaningful abstract formal theory of rational behavior.

Nevertheless, it seems desirable that we begin our discussion with some abstract theory of behavior in order to appreciate

[1] B. Russell, "Can Men Be Rational?" Ch. IV in *Sceptical Essays*, Unwin Books, London, 1960, p. 32.
[2] R. D. Luce and H. Raiffa, *Games and Decisions*, John Wiley, New York, 1957, p. 5.
[3] K. E. Boulding, *Conflict and Defense*, Harper and Brothers, New York, 1962, p. 9.

these difficulties. Consequently, suppose that individual behavior satisfies the following postulates:

(i) At any point of time, the individual has an image[4] of his *possible* acts and the *possible* outcomes from adopting them.

(ii) He orders these acts in logical consistency with his preferences[5] over outcome possibilities. This ordering is assumed to be transitive and complete.[6]

(iii) He acts consistently with this ordering.

A theory of behavior exhibiting this degree of internal consistency might be said to describe rational behavior.[7]

Such a theory, however, is not very stringent in its assumptions, since it merely requires that an individual act in logical consistency with his preference ordering of perceived possibilities. One may, indeed, wish to impose stricter conditions. For example, in addition to consistency as defined above, one

[4] No theory of image formation will be given in this analysis. It seems to me that a serious complication is involved in traditional outlines of rational behavior. The images are assumed not to depend upon the individual's aims or strength of motivation but to be related to his body of knowledge. But there is little doubt that in many cases both factors play a role and that it is reasonable for an individual to vary his image depending upon his aims, e.g. to specify the possibilities more closely or less so. The interdependence of aims and images creates difficulties for theories which attempt to consider these independently. For a general discussion of the role of images in behavior see K. E. Boulding, *The Image*, The University of Michigan Press, Ann Arbor, 1956. For an outline of theories of the formation of anticipated price images by the firm, see Edwin S. Mills, *Price, Output, and Inventory Policy*, John Wiley, New York, 1962, Ch. 3, "The Analysis of Expectations."

[5] Much legitimate metaphysical debate is possible as to what this ordering represents or ought to represent. One may assert that it corresponds with the individual's anticipated level of anticipated satisfaction. But the individual may be uncertain in the anticipation of this, and his anticipated values may differ from actual ones even supposing that satisfaction can be identified.

[6] The assumptions of the completeness of the ordering and its transitivity everywhere are stronger than required to ensure that an individual selects his most preferred act. This will be elaborated when Simon's objections to "orthodox" decision theory are discussed below.

[7] In this case, no test of the "reasonableness" of the images is involved. The image merely indicates the acts and outcomes which the individual thinks or *believes* are possible.

may wish to impose the condition that the images are logically consistent with the individual's knowledge or, in a looser sense, are reasonable given *his* knowledge. Even more stringent tests of rationality can be imagined but, in this analysis, I shall limit the test to the type of consistency of the above theory. Further progress can be made by outlining a formal version of the above theory.

B. A Rational Decision Theory

A formal version of the above broad theory of (rational) behavior is obtained by making the following assumptions:

(i) At any point of time, the individual imagines that there is some set of alternative acts A° which are available for his choice. If A represents the set of alternative acts available to the individual, it will be assumed that $A^\circ \subseteq A$.

(ii) The individual associates a set of possible outcomes, O°, with the set of possible acts, A°. With each act he associates a set of outcome possibilities. We represent the set of outcome possibilities attaching to ith act by O°_i. For example, in some cases the elements of O°_i consist of ordered pairs which indicate the probability of profit which the individual associates with the act A°_i. Where ρ represents the probability with which the individual anticipates the profit, π, O°_i might contain the elements $(\pi_1, \rho_1), (\pi_2, \rho_2), \ldots, (\pi_n, \rho_n)$.

(iii) The individual has a preference ordering over the O°_i sets, and these meet the usual consistency requirements of transitivity and symmetry.[8]

An individual's action is rational if he adopts an act A°_k,

[8] Behavior may be rational even if the ordering of the set O° is not complete and even if intransitive and non-symmetric orderings arise for some members of the set. Suppose that all elements of some proper subset J of O° are *known* to be preferred to all elements of O° which are not members of this subset. Now, it will always be rational to choose an act corresponding to an outcome possibility in J, and the ordering of elements in the set $O^\circ - J$ is irrelevant to the problem *given* the above knowledge. Incomplete orderings or inconsistencies of elements in the set $O^\circ - J$ need not prevent rational behavior. Such gaps, may, indeed, be optimal given some types of maximizing behavior.

whose set of possible outcomes O°_k is no less preferred by him than the set for any act contained in A°. If there are $i = 1$, ..., m alternative acts contained in A°, the individual selects an act A°_k such that

$$U(O^\circ_k) \geq U(O^\circ_i), \ i = 1, \ldots, m,$$

and where U is an index of preference over the O°_i sets. The index is defined such that if any set of outcome possibilities O°_g is preferred to another set O°_f, then $U(O^\circ_g) > U(O^\circ_f)$; if O°_g is equally preferred to O°_f, then $U(O^\circ_g) = U(O^\circ_f)$; and if O°_g is less preferred than O°_f, $U(O^\circ_g) < U(O^\circ_f)$.

C. Some Problems and Consequences
of this Decision Theory

In the above theory, there is no part concerned with the formation of images. They are taken as datum, and search and learning behavior is not discussed. Clearly, the individual's aims and costs involved in the collection of information and the process of reaching a decision are not unimportant in influencing the collection of information and the trouble taken over the decision process itself. In many circumstances, it is "optimal" to collect little information and come to a decision by rough-and-ready means.[9]

[9] E. S. Mills argues that there is no reason to despair about the empirical relevance of the principle that people behave "as if" they are employing some criterion of rational choice "if we do not forget that part of a rational decision is the rational consideration of what resources to invest in the collection of information and the computation of the decision." In other words, he suggests that an allowance be made for a rational choice of the decision process itself. But ought not this choice be rational, and so on, and where do the ultimate limits to rationality occur, if they do? The points which Mills touches on are important, but his formulation is too vague to enable us to resolve any dilemmas, since he defines rationality in the following way: "Vaguely, the concept of rationality involves doing the best you can in the circumstances to get what you want." This is a loose and unclear definition. See, E. S. Mills, *op. cit.*, Ch. 2, "Rationality and the 'As If' Principles."

Baumol and Quandt have given specific instances in which limited orderings and attenuated decision rules are optimal. See W. J. Baumol and R. E. Quandt, "Rules of Thumb and Optimally Imperfect Decisions," *American Economic Review*, vol. 54 (1964), pp. 23–46.

It is supposed above that $A°$ is a subset of A, but, since $A°$ is only imagined, cases may arise where $A°$ is not a subset of A. The above theory does not describe what happens if the individual tries to adopt an act outside the set A. It is also clear, if $A°$ is a proper subset of A, that the individual may choose an act which is less preferable than another available but unknown one and that the individual may not act rationally due to inconsistencies or incompleteness in his ordering of $A°$. Finally, we may not be able to view the set of available alternative acts as being certain but only as probable.[10] Yet despite these limitations, a rational decision theory of the above form has been widely employed in economic theory[11] and has shown sufficient correspondence with observed events to give us some insight into them.

D. Possibilities and
Probability Weights

The above rational decision theory suggests that in some circumstances individuals may assign probability weights to different possible outcomes, and this raises the question of how individuals decide upon what is possible and how they assign probability weights. More generally, it raises the question of how individuals specify their uncertainty about variables. I do not believe that individuals always assign cardinal probability weights to their possibilities and manipulate them so as to satisfy the axioms of probability. Uncertainty is specified in a large variety of ways, and it is a challenge to our wits to allow for this. Nevertheless, I believe that probability weights, or something akin to them, play an important role in much decision-making under uncertainty.

Now probability weights can be given and have been given many different interpretations. But for some purposes, it is sufficient to know that they can be identified and that they

---

[10] If this situation arises, there may be no act which ensures Pareto optimality, and the above representation of rational behavior does not cover the case. See C. Tisdell, "Some Bounds upon the Pareto Optimality of Group Behavior," *Kyklos*, vol. 19 (1966), pp. 81–105.

[11] Cf. K. E. Boulding, *Conflict and Defense*, p. 9.

enter into the decision in a particular way. For example, one may wish to assume that probabilities satisfy a set of mathematical axioms of probability[12] and that they influence the ordering in a particular way. Depending upon the circumstances, these weights can be given a personalistic or an objective interpretation. Both the relative frequency and the logical probability views attempt to assign an "objective" interpretation to probability weights. To get some impression of the range of possible interpretations, let us briefly consider some theories of probability.

Venn,[13] Richard von Mises,[14] and Reichenbach[15] argue that probability is based upon relative frequency. For von Mises, the probability of an event is the relative frequency of its occurrence as the number of trials tends to infinity. Von Mises maintains that ". . . in order to apply the theory of probability we must have a practically unlimited sequence of uniform observations."[16] Reichenbach claims a wider range of application for the relative frequency approach than does von Mises. While Reichenbach retains the infinite sequence formulation [17] of von Mises, he takes account of the fact that actual

[12] Kolmogorov states a set of such axioms, and his general views on probability seem most commendable. Broadly, his axioms are as follows: Let E be a collection of elements and $\mathscr{H}$ a set of the subsets of E.

  I. $\mathscr{H}$ is a field of sets.
  II. $\mathscr{H}$ contains the set E.
  III. To each set A in $\mathscr{H}$ is assigned a non-negative real number $P(A)$ called the probability of the event A.
  IV. $P(E)$ equals 1.
  V. If A and B have no element in common,

$$P(A + B) = P(A) + P(B)$$

A. N. Kolmogorov, *Foundations of the Theory of Probability*, Chelsea Publishing Company, New York, 1950. Measures with other properties could also be assigned to members of the set. There is no unique set of mathematical axioms of probability.

[13] J. Venn, *Logic of Chance*, 2nd edn., Macmillan, London, 1876.

[14] R. von Mises, *Probability, Statistics and Truth*, 2nd edn., George Allen and Unwin, London, 1957.

[15] H. Reichenbach, *The Theory of Probability*, University of California Press, Berkeley, 1949.

[16] von Mises, *op. cit.*, p. 11.

[17] Reichenbach, *op. cit.*, pp. 344–346.

sequences are finite, so that the best that can be hoped for is a convergence of relative frequency in a finite interval. Reichenbach considers unique cases in terms of "posits" or probability weights and links these weights with frequencies.[18] For example, it may be possible to relate the probability that some unique event has occurred to the frequency of reports of its occurrence.

A different view of probability has been presented by J. M. Keynes,[19] H. Jeffreys,[20] and R. Carnap.[21] For Keynes, "the terms *certain* and *probable* describe the various degrees of rational belief about a proposition which different amounts of knowledge authorise us to entertain."[22] It is the essence of Keynes' approach that probability expresses a relationship. Given the knowledge to which the probability of a conclusion is to be related, it is rational to entertain a certain degree of belief, and no other degree of belief, as to the truth of the conclusion. It is held that the appropriate rational degree of belief and, therefore, the appropriate level of probability can be deduced by logical methods. This formulation is held to be independent of the individual and to be true "to the outside world."

Ramsey[23] has objected to Keynes' contention that there is but one probability which it is rational to infer in any given state of knowledge. Ramsey,[24] De Finetti,[25] and Savage[26]

[18] *Ibid.*, pp. 372–378.

[19] J. M. Keynes, *A Treatise on Probability*, Macmillan, London 1921.

[20] H. Jeffreys, *Theory of Probability*, 2nd edn., The Clarendon Press, Oxford, 1948.

[21] R. Carnap, *Logical Foundations of Probability*, The University of Chicago, Chicago, 1950. Also, for an analysis of Carnap's theory, G. Tintner, "Foundations of Probability and Statistical Inference," *Journal of the Royal Statistical Society*, Vol. 112 (1949), Part III, pp. 251–279.

[22] Keynes, *op. cit.*, p. 3.

[23] F. P. Ramsey, "Truth and Probability" (1926), essay VII (pp. 157–198) in *The Foundations of Mathematics and Other Logical Essays*, R. Braithwaite, ed., Routledge and Kegan Paul, London, 1931.

[24] *Ibid.*

[25] B. De Finetti, "La prévision: ses lois logiques, ses sources subjectives," *Annales de l'Institut Henri Poincaré*, vol. 7 (1937), pp. 1–68.

[26] L. J. Savage, *The Foundations of Statistics*, John Wiley, New York, 1954.

take a personalistic view of probability. They argue that it is rational for different individuals to hold different probabilities upon the basis of the same evidence. This approach is concerned with those probabilities which the individual *ought* to hold if there is to be logical consistency between his expressed opinions and preferences. It is *not* concerned with those probabilities which the individual ought to hold in relation to his body of knowledge.[27] In the personalistic approach, probabilities are expressed in numerical terms by considering the extent to which an individual is prepared to act as indicated by the amounts he is willing to wager. The approach is based upon a simple set of behavior axioms.[28] If these axioms hold, decision weights which satisfy the probability theory rules are discoverable, and the individual's utility allowances are measurable up to a linear transform.

Fellner[29] suggests that individuals may assign decision weights which do not satisfy the usual rules of probability theory, for they may "slant" probabilities so as to allow for the possibility of disappointment. If E indicates an event and if $\bar{E}$ indicates its complement and if $P_D(E)$ indicates the decision weight placed on the event E and if $P_D(\bar{E})$ indicates the decision weight placed by the individual on its complement, it is possible that $P_D(E) + P_D(\bar{E}) < 1$. It remains true that the objective probability of the event's occurring or not occurring is one.

Clearly, decision weights can be assigned many different interpretations, the traditional mathematical axioms of probability need not be satisfied by all, and no generally best form of interpretation can be given. But probability weights which satisfy the traditional mathematical axioms exhibit internal logical consistency and, given some meanings, correspond

[27] These personal probabilities may be inconsistent with the logical probabilities or with the true relative frequencies appropriate to the circumstance. Cf. Ramsey, *op. cit.*, p. 82.

[28] For a statement of these axioms, see Savage, *op. cit.*

[29] William Fellner, *Probability and Profit*, Richard D. Irwin, Homewood, Ill., 1965. The reader who requires a more detailed study of probability than the one given above will find Fellner's work valuable.

with phenomena which are observable in principle.[30] They demarcate an important ideal type and will be used in this analysis.

E. The Relationship between Criteria and the above Theory of Rational Behavior

Sometimes an individual's preference ordering indicates that his rational behavior ought to be in accordance with a simple rule or criterion. His rational behavior is in accordance with a rule or criterion if the consistent application of that rule or criterion leads to the selection of an act A_k such that $U(O^\circ_k) \geq U(O^\circ_i)$, where $i = 1, \ldots, m$. The rule which is applied to the set O° may be a multi-stage one. For example, its first stage may involve an operation on O° to construct a new set $\hat{O}^\circ$. An operation may then be performed on the set $\hat{O}^\circ$ to select the rational act. For instance, the maximin criterion, which will be discussed later, can be applied directly to O° to select an act, or it may be used as a second-stage rule in a criterion such as the following one: "Maximin" upon the basis of the possible profit values which have a probability of occurrence of greater than 0.001. This criterion involves the following two stages:

(i) Select from the set of possible profit values associated with each act those profit values which have a probability of occurrence of greater than 0.001. Let these values form a set $\hat{\pi}$.

(ii) On the basis of the set $\hat{\pi}$, solve for the maximin level of profit.

In introducing some decision criteria, I shall assume that they apply to the set O° and are not a stage in a more general rule which is applied to O° to select an act. The criteria will be divided into two groups: one which is dependent upon cardinal probabilities and one which is not. In the former group, we shall include (1) expected profit maximization; (2) expected utility maximization; (3) criteria relying upon a preference

[30] Cf. Kolmogorov, *op. cit.*, pp. 2–3.

of first and second moments of the choice variables, and even higher moments; (4) the maximization of a preference functional over the total shape of the probability functions attaching to the variables; and (5) some probability of loss criteria. Included in the latter group are (1) Shackle's psychological theory; (2) the minimax rule; (3) the maximax rule; (4) Hurwicz's criterion; and (5) Savage's regret criterion. Let us discuss each of these criteria in turn.

F. Decision Criteria which Rely on Cardinal Probability Weights

1. *The expected gain (profit) maximization criterion*.[31] If p_j is the probability of the occurrence of the jth state of nature where there are n possible alternative states, and if a_{ij} represents the individual's monetary gain if he adopts his ith act or strategy and the jth state of nature prevails, then his expected gain from his ith act or strategy is

$$E_i = \sum_{j=1}^{n} p_j a_{ij} \qquad (i = 1, \ldots, m).$$

In this case, the individual's optimal act is considered to be one which maximizes his expected gain, i.e., one which maximizes E_i.

The weights p_j used in the index E_i are assumed to satisfy the usual axioms of probability. However, they may well have different values depending upon the type of interpretation which we wish to give, i.e., they may be relative frequencies, subjective values, etc.[32] But whatever the interpretation, the

---

[31] Marschak calls this the Bayes criterion. See J. Marschak, "Probability in the Social Sciences," pp. 166–215 in *Mathematical Thinking in the Social Sciences*, P. L. Lazersfeld, ed., The Free Press, Glencoe Ill., 1954. Also, see Thomas Bayes, "An Essay Towards Solving a Problem in the Doctrine of Chances," reprinted in *Biometrika*, vol. 45, parts 3 and 4, pp. 293–315.

[32] In the special case where one is "completely" ignorant it has been suggested, upon the basis of the so-called principle of insufficient reason, that the individual should assign equal probabilities to each possible "event." In the above case where there are n distinct possible "states of

criterion implies that the preference ordering of acts depends *only* upon the "first moment" of the money prize. The "spread" of the possible gains or losses is assumed not to influence the individual's preference for any act. However, there are clearly cases where moments other than the first, and other aspects of the distribution of possibilities, influence the individual's choice of acts.

2. *The expected utility maximization criterion.* Assuming utility to be cardinal, let u_{ij} represent the utility which the individual attaches to the outcome of his ith act when the jth state of nature occurs. We suppose that the individual considers that $i = 1, \ldots, m$ alternative acts are available to him and that $j = 1, \ldots, n$ alternative states of nature are possible. The individual's expected utility from his ith act is then given by

$$E(u_i) = \sum_{j=1}^{n} \rho_j u_{ij} \qquad (i = 1, \ldots, m)$$

This rule states that the optimal act is the one which maximizes expected utility, i.e., the one for which $E(u_i)$ is at a maximum.

This rule was suggested by Daniel Bernouilli[33] as early as 1738. He assumed that utility was cardinally measurable and claimed that an individual should maximize his moral expectation or expected utility. Given such a view, the individual should only maximize his expected gain if his utility varies linearly with the money prize. In those circumstances, the individual will certainly maximize his expected utility by maximizing his expected gain, but if his gain is subject to diminishing or increasing marginal utility, the expected gain rule will not maximize his expected utility.

---

nature," this rule indicates that $\rho_j = 1/n$, where $j = 1, \ldots, n$. The expected gain criterion based upon this rule is sometimes referred to as the Laplace criterion. A certain amount of arbitrariness arises for the ρ_j values in this rule if the division of possibilities is arbitrary.

[33] Daniel Bernouilli, "Specimen theoriae novae de mensura sortis," *Comentari academiae scientarum imperialis Petropolitanae*, Vol. 5 (1738), pp. 175–192. Translated by Dr. Louise Sommer, as "Exposition of a New Theory on the Measurement of Risk," *Econometrica*, vol. 12 (1954), pp. 23–36.

For Bernouilli, the cardinality of utility was only an assumption. Ramsey[34] and von Neumann and Morgenstern[35] have been able to show that cardinality of utility follows from the assumption of a small number of simple axioms.[36] Von Neumann and Morgenstern demonstrate that if these axioms are fulfilled then utility is measurable up to a linear transform. Savage[37] and Markowitz[38] have shown that if the individual accepts the von Neumann and Morgenstern utility axioms then, to be consistent, he must act so as to maximize his expected utility. Logically, expected utility maximization is the only criterion consistent with these utility axioms.

A number of writers reject criteria such as the maximin gain, minimax regret, maximax gain, and Hurwicz rules, since the behavior which they imply is not always consistent with expected utility behavior.[39] They imply behavior which is inconsistent with the utility axioms. But this assumes that the utility axioms are the only relevant and adequate ones. Their adequacy is questionable. In particular, the utility axiom of

[34] Ramsey, *op. cit.*

[35] J. von Neumann and O. Morgenstern, *Theory of Games and Economic Behavior*, Princeton University Press, Princèton, 1st edn., 1944, esp. pp. 16–29; 3rd edn., 1953.

[36] If we let ">" indicate "preferred to" and "=" designate "indifferent to," these axioms are as follows:

Axiom Ia: If P and Q are two probability distributions of outcomes then either $P > Q$, or $Q > P$, or $P = Q$. (Completeness in the ordering or "comparability.")

Axiom Ib: If $P \geq Q$ and $Q \geq R$, then $P \geq R$. ("transitivity").

Axiom II: If $P > Q$ and R is a probability distribution of an outcome then, $aP + (1 - a)R > aQ + (1 - a)R$, given $a > 0$.

Axiom III: If $P > Q$ and $Q > R$ then there is a number c such that $cP + (1 - c)R = Q$ where $0 < c < 1$. ("continuity").

These axioms imply the measurability of utility up to a linear transform. They do not imply that utility can be added for different individuals, but merely provide the individual with a numerical ordering system. These axioms are discussed in detail by Markowitz. H. M. Markowitz, *Portfolio Selection—Efficient Diversifications of Investments*, John Wiley, New York, 1959, esp. pp. 229–234.

[37] Savage, *op. cit.*, pp. 70–76 and p. 105.

[38] Markowitz, *op. cit.*, pp. 235–242.

[39] For instance, Markowitz does.

continuity is dubious. This is the axiom that if there are three possible outcomes, P, Q, and R, and the individual prefers P to Q to R, then there is some probable value of P and R such that he is indifferent between a lottery involving them and the certainty of Q. But the individual may, if he has the choice, be unprepared to participate in a lottery in which a possible outcome could involve him in starvation, bankruptcy, or a tremendous fall in social status. Since such behavior is neither completely unreasonable nor unlikely to occur[40] there are insufficient grounds for rejecting criteria which do not satisfy the utility axioms.

Now, depending upon the form of the utility function, the maximization of expected utility rule becomes expressable in terms of other rules. For instance, if utility is a linear function of money payoff π, expected utility is a linear function of the expected value of π. If

$$u = a + b\pi,$$

then

$$E[u] = a + bE[\pi],$$

and $E[u]$ is at a maximum when $E[\pi]$ attains its maximum possible value. Again, if u is a quadratic function of π, $E[u]$ depends only upon the mean and variance of π. If

$$u = a + b\pi + c\pi^2,$$

then

$$E[u] = a + bE[\pi] + cE[\pi^2]$$
$$= a + bE[\pi] + c(E[\pi])^2 + c \text{ var } [\pi].$$

In this case, preferences depend in a *particular way* upon the first and the second moment of the gain. More generally, if u is a polynomial function of π in the Nth degree, then expected utility can be expressed as a linear function of the

---

[40] Arrow takes the opposite view. See K. J. Arrow, *Aspects of the Theory of Risk-Bearing*, Yrjö Jahnsson Lectures, The Academic Book-store, Helsinki, 1965, p. 15. For other *important* limitations of the utility axioms see von Neumann and Morgenstern, *op. cit.*, 3rd edn., pp.628–632.

first N moments of the distribution of π. Other simple relationships also exist depending upon the form of u.[41]

3. *Preference orderings over the moments of the payoff.* These preference orderings may refer to any number of moments. They may refer to the mean alone, to the mean and the variance, or to all possible moments. From the set of moments available to him, the individual is assumed to select an act which gives him his most preferable moment combination. Marschak[42] has envisaged the firm as a unit having a preference ordering over all of the moments of the probability distribution of such variates as profits and the value of assets and suggests that it will attempt to maximize its utility functional for these moments subject to its technical restrictions. One problem with such a general theory is that it gives no indication of the relative significance of different parameters, and it may involve serious abstractions about the ability of individuals to grasp and order possibilities. Exponents of this approach do not necessarily assume cardinality of utility.

4. *The maximization of a preference functional over the total shape of the probability functions attaching to the payoffs.* Tinter[43] has suggested this rule and it is subject to the same type of drawbacks as the above one of Marschak's.

[41] Entirely due to the convexity or concavity of the function some simple inequalities hold. If the function is analytic it can generally be approximated by a polynomial function by using Taylor's theorem, and then its expected value can be approximated by calculating the expected value of the polynomial. If the polynomial is of the Nth degree, this calculation will involve the first N moments of its dependent variables. Other simple approximations and functional relationships can arise. For a limited taxonomy of these, see R. Radner, "Mathematical Specifications of Goals for Decision Problems," Ch. 11 in *Human Judgments and Optimality,* M. W. Shelly and G. Bryan, eds., John Wiley, New York, 1964.

[42] J. Marschak, (i) "Utilities and Probabilities in Human Choice," an abstract in *Report of Third Annual Research Conference on Economics and Statistics,* Colorado Springs, 1937, pp. 79–82. (ii) "Money and the Theory of Assets," *Econometrica,* vol. 6 (1938), pp. 311–325.

[43] G. Tintner, "A contribution to the Nonstatic Theory of Production," pp. 92–109 in *Studies in Mathematical Economics and Econometrics,* O. Lange, F. McIntyre, and T. O. Yntema, eds., University of Chicago Press, Chicago, 1942.

5. *Probability of loss criteria.* Several economists have argued that negative returns are of particular concern to the firm, and they suggest that these returns should enter specifically into some decision criteria. Domar and Musgrave[44] have suggested that the most preferable policy might be selected from a preference ordering over the expected total gains and expected losses of different policies. This approach ignores the dispersion of losses. A. D. Roy[45] argues that "safety first" is the guiding principle of the firm and, consequently, that it wishes to minimize the probability of a disaster level of income. Clearly, a firm which acts on this principle exhibits a morbid preoccupation with loss. If one is trying to characterize the behavior of most firms it is probably more realistic to suppose that a firm wishes to maximize its expected profit provided that its action gives it some satisfactory assurance (probability) that it will not fail or obtain an income less than a particular crucial figure.[46]

G. Criteria Which do not
Rely on Cardinal Probabilities

1. *Shackle's psychological theory.* G. L. S. Shackle[47] criticizes the application of cardinal probability estimates to decision-making under uncertainty. He argues that it is impossible to calculate relative frequencies for many economic occurrences because they are unique and non-repetitive. Although this is so, it may still be the case that in some circumstances decision-makers do assign cardinal weights to the possible outcomes. We may, if we wish, call these weights

[44] E. Domar and R. Musgrave, "Proportional Income Taxation and Risk-Taking," *Quarterly Journal of Economics*, vol. 58 (1944), pp. 388–422.

[45] A. D. Roy, "Safety First and the Holding of Assets," *Econometrica*, vol. 20 (1952), pp. 431–449.

[46] For a detailed development of this view, see C. Tisdell, "Decision Making and the Probability of Loss," *Australian Economic Papers*, vol. 1 (1962), pp. 109–118.

[47] G. L. S. Shackle: (i) *Expectation in Economics*, The University Press, Cambridge, 1949. (ii) *Uncertainty in Economics*, The University Press, Cambridge, 1955. (iii) *Time in Economics*, North-Holland Publishing Company, Amsterdam, 1958.

cardinal probabilities. Shackle doubts the widespread use of such weights. He suggests that the individual assesses the uncertainty of the possible outcomes in terms of potential surprise. The potential surprise function ordinally represents the degree to which an individual would be surprised by various outcomes. By considering the potential surprise function along with a function representing the degree of "interestingness," focus values, and a gambler indifference system, Shackle formulates his rule for choice under uncertainty. The degree-of-interestingness function depends ordinally on potential surprise and the value of the possible outcomes. The primary focus values for any scheme (act) are determined from the points of tangency of the potential surprise function and the contours of the degree-of-interestingness function. These primary focus values are standardized and are transferred to the gambler's indifference map. From this map the optimal scheme (act) is determined. This scheme is the one having the most preferred set of standardized focus values in the set of attainable values.

Mostly, Shackle's model yields two focus values. While it is agreed that the individual may only give active consideration to a restricted set of values, it seems unduly restrictive to suppose him to focus his attention upon two. While Shackle's model seems to have a psychological counterpart, it is nevertheless fundamentally indeterminate, for it does not yield *unique* standardized focus values. If *both* the degree of potential surprise and the degree of interestingness are taken as pure rankings, then the potential surprise function and the degree-of-interestingness function fail to take up unique positions. In consequence, the focus and standardized values are not unique. Shackle's situation is analogous to trying to maximize an ordinal function (in this case the degree of interestingness) subject to an ordinal restriction (in this case the potential surprise function); the solution is indeterminate.[48]

[48] Cf. C. Carter, p. 53 in *Uncertainty and Business Decisions*, eds. C. F. Carter, G. P. Meredith, and G. L. S. Shackle, eds., The University Press, Liverpool, 1954.

THEORY OF PRICE UNCERTAINTY

2. *The maximin or Wald criterion.* According to this criterion, the individual wishes to ensure himself of a payoff which is no less than the maximum of the minimum possible payoffs for the acts in $A°$. Let the payoffs be in terms of money values. Then, if a_{ij} represents the individual's money payoff for the ith act when the jth state of nature prevails, the maximin act is one which corresponds to

$$\text{Max Min } a_{ij}.$$
$$\ \ \ \ \ i \ \ \ \ j$$

The rule stated here is for pure and not mixed strategies.

A slightly different rule is the maximin expected gain rule. The optimal act according to this rule is one which ensures the agent of at least the maximum of the least possible *expected* gains for different strategies. This criterion can involve mixed strategies. *If the firm adopts a mixed strategy, it runs the risk of obtaining less than the maximum of its least possible gains.*[49]

[49] To be more specific, let $A° = \{\alpha_1, \ldots, \alpha_m\}$ represent the firm's set of pure strategies. If only pure strategies are allowed, the problem is to choose an act from this set which ensures the payoff $v^* = \text{Max Min } a_{ij}$.
If mixed strategies are allowed, the maximin expected gain criterion can be viewed as one of choosing an optimal probability vector defined on the space of pure strategies, i.e., of choosing an optimal vector $[\rho_1, \ldots, \rho_m]$, where $\sum_{i=1}^{m} \rho_i = 1$ and $O \le \rho_i \le 1$. If v represents the maximin expected gain value, $v \ge v^*$. Allowing mixed strategies, let $C = \{\alpha'_1, \ldots, \alpha'_k\}$ represent the acts which, given the use of *optimal* probability vector, have a positive probability of choice. Let there be $r = 1, \ldots, k$ acts in C. $C \subset A°$ and $k \le m$. Then, if

$$\text{Min Min } a_{rj} < \text{Max Min } a_{ij}$$
$$\ \ r \ \ \ j \ \ \ \ \ \ \ \ i \ \ \ j$$

and the firm adopts a minimax *expected* gain policy, it runs the risk of obtaining less than the maximum of its least possible gains.

To give an example, suppose that the firm or player has two alternative pure strategies and that there are two possible states of nature. $A° = \{\alpha_1, \alpha_2\}$ and $S = \{s_1, s_2\}$ and the matrix of payoffs is $[a_{ij}]$ where $i = 1, 2$ and $j = 1, 2$. If $a_{21} < a_{12} < a_{11} < a_{22}$, the minimax (pure) strategy is a_{12}, but the minimax mixed strategy involves a probability weighting of the two acts. This weighting makes a_{21} possible, and a_{21} is less than a_{12}. An example of this case is illustrated in the following diagram. Pure strategies alone being allowed act α_1 gives the minimax value of v^*. If mixed strategies are permitted, the minimax expected gain strategy

30

With mixed strategies the rationale for a maximin strategy, i.e., to make sure of at least a certain minimum gain, disappears. If any individual is prepared to run a risk by adopting a mixed strategy, then we would not be surprised if he really wished to maximize expected gain (or utility) because the security aspect becomes almost insignificant in the maximin expected gain approach.

Sometimes an analogy is drawn between situations in which the maximin expected gain criterion is applied and situations involving zero-sum two-person games.[50] The economic agent (firm, statistician, etc.) is assumed to be opposed by a fictitious player, Nature. Nature has a number of strategies available to it, and the economic agent has a number of acts open to it. The outcome for both parties will be determined by their simultaneous strategies. The analogy cannot be pressed very far because complete correspondence requires

   (i) the utility gains of the economic agent to be equal to the utility losses of Nature and

---

gives a value of v and involves the choice of α_1 with a probability of ρ°_1 and α_2 with a probability of $1 - \rho^{\circ}_1 > 0$. In this case, the worst possibility

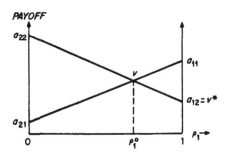

may occur, viz., a payoff of a_{21}. Those who are unfamiliar with the above diagram might consult E. S. Venttsel', *An Introduction to the Theory of Games*, D. C. Heath & Co., Boston, 1963.

(ii) Nature to be an active opponent minimizing its maximum level of expected loss.

In addition, the economic agent must attempt to maximize its minimum level of expected gain. As shown by von Neumann and Morgenstern,[51] a stable solution for a zero-sum two-person game will either exist for unmixed or mixed strategies. In these circumstances, there is no inconsistency between the utility axioms and the use of the maximin criterion because, if Nature always adopts its minimax loss strategy, the firm will always maximize its expected utility by adopting its maximin act. One can object to the above formulation because it assumes Nature to be an active opponent. If Nature is a passive opponent, use of the maximin criterion can be inconsistent with the von Neumann–Morgenstern utility axioms. If the economic agent has some knowledge of the probabilities with which Nature "plays" its strategies, then its expected utility can be greatest for a non-maximin act. Hence, a divergency arises between the maximin rule and the expected utility maxim. If one is going to apply the maximin rule in such circumstances, logical consistency requires that one reject the von Neumann–Morgenstern utility axioms and the associated utility index.

The maximin gain criterion (also called the Wald or minimax loss criterion)[52] is, if limited to pure strategies, extremely conservative. It is consistent with the preference ordering of an individual who is not prepared to take a risk. It is so security biased that we rarely expect it to be applied to the set of possibilities $O°$.

3. *The maximax criterion.* The maximax stands at the opposite end of the gambling spectrum to the minimax. The

---

[50] A. Wald, *Statistical Decision Functions*, John Wiley, New York, 1950, pp. 26–27.

[51] Von Neumann and Morgenstern, *op. cit.*

[52] J. Milnor, "Games Against Nature," pp. 49–59 in *Decision Processes*, edited by R. M. Thrall, C. H. Coombs and R. L. Davis, John Wiley, New York, 1954.

individual bases his decision entirely upon the best possible payoff. The agent's optimal maximax policy is the one for

$$\text{Max}_i \text{ Max}_j \; a_{ij}$$

When applied to the set $O°$ it implies an extreme type of gambling behavior.

4. *The Hurwicz criterion.* The Hurwicz criterion[53] is based upon a weighting of the greatest and least possible gain for each act. A fixed number β, which reflects the agent's pessimism, is attached to the least possible gain for each act and an optimism weight $1 - \beta$ is attached to the greatest possible gain for each act. Given that $0 \leq \beta \leq 1$, an index,

$$H_i = \beta \; \text{Min}_j \; a_{ij} + (1 - \beta) \; \text{Max}_j \; a_{ij},$$

is computed for each act. The optimal Hurwicz act is the one which maximizes this index, i.e., the one for which

$$\text{Max}_i \; [\beta \; \text{Min}_j \; a_{ij} + (1 - \beta) \; \text{Max}_j \; a_{ij}]$$

occurs. If $\beta = 1$ this criterion is equivalent to the Wald criterion, and if $\beta = 0$ it is equivalent to the maximax. The Hurwicz criterion focuses attention upon the best and worst possible outcomes for each act to the exclusion of all others. It is possible to develop criteria which besides giving special weights to the extremes also give weights to other values.

5. *The Savage regret criterion.* Prior to his presentation of the personalistic probability theory of expected utility maximization, Savage suggested a regret criterion[54] which allowed for the alternative which is possibly foregone by selecting one act in preference to another. Originally, this criterion

[53] L. Hurwicz, "Optimality Criteria for Decision Making under Ignorance," Cowles Commission Discussion Paper, No. 370, 1950. Mimeographed.
[54] L. J. Savage: "The Theory of Statistical Decision," *Journal of the American Statistical Association*, vol. 46 (1951), pp. 55–67.

was in terms of utilities. Let u_{ij} be the utility for the outcome of the ith act and the jth state of nature. Then a regret matrix $[r_{ij}]$, with the elements

$$r_{ij} = \operatorname{Max}_{j} u_{ij} - u_{ij}$$

indicates the possible regrets. The firm's aim is to ensure that its regret does not exceed the minimum of the maximum possible regret values for the acts. Its optimal act corresponds to

$$\operatorname*{Min}_{i} \operatorname*{Max}_{j} r_{ij}.$$

As Chernoff[55] suggests, it is by no means apparent that regret ought to be measured by differences in utility or that it should vary linearly with such differences.

H. An Additional Limitation of Some of These Criteria

An additional and obvious limitation of the Wald, maximax, Hurwicz, and Savage regret criteria might be mentioned. They do not always correctly order possibilities. They violate the principle that if the vector of possible payoffs from any one act exceeds that for another, then the former is preferred. Consider the following case in which there are three possible states of nature and two alternative acts. For the payoffs shown in the body of the matrix, the Wald and Hurwicz criteria violate the principle. Act α_2 is the most preferable act, but the Wald and Hurwicz criteria suggest that the individual is indifferent between the alternative acts.

$$
\begin{array}{cc}
 & \begin{array}{ccc} s_1 & s_2 & s_3 \end{array} \\
\begin{array}{c} \alpha_1 \\ \alpha_2 \end{array} & \begin{bmatrix} 4 & 1 & 1 \\ 4 & 10 & 1 \end{bmatrix}
\end{array}
$$

Similarly, if a_{22}, the payoff from the second act when the strategy s_2 prevails, happens to be in the range $1 < a_{22} \leq 4$

[55] H. Chernoff: "Rational Selection of Decision Functions," *Econometrica*, vol. 22 (1954), pp. 442–443.

and if the other payoff values remain as above, the Hurwicz and maximax criteria rank the acts equally. However, in fact, α_2 is the most preferable act. Examples can also be constructed to show that the Savage regret criterion violates this principle.[56] Criteria such as Bayes' and Laplace's, which rely upon weighted overall values, do not violate it.

As Milnor[57] points out, a minor modification enables inconsistencies of this sort to be eliminated. To overcome this type of inconsistency, we eliminate all dominated strategies from the original decision matrix and can then apply the above criteria to the resultant matrix of payoffs. If all vectorial domination is strong, the above problems do not occur. They can only arise if weak domination is present.

I. Some Passing Observations

Objective circumstances remaining the same, rational behavior can be extremely diverse. All other things remaining unchanged, variations in the preference orderings of individuals and in their state of knowledge can lead to great variation in their chosen *rational* acts. This is because rationality is judged in relation to the individual's preference ordering and his state of knowledge. If, in reality, these two factors tend to vary from individual to individual or for the same individual over time, there may be considerable diversity in behavior and yet behavior may be rational.

In the same objective circumstances, different criteria can be consistent with rational choice,[58] differences arising due to variations in knowledge and preference orderings. Despite the fact that two individuals have identical preference orderings and face the same objective circumstances, differences in

[56] For an example, see Milnor, *op. cit.*

[57] Milnor, *op. cit.*, fn. 4.

[58] It is assumed above that a criterion is consistent with rational behavior if it leads to the choice of the "most preferred" act in the set A°. This is a weak requirement. A more stringent one, which is not adopted here, is as follows: A criterion is only consistent with rational behavior if, no matter what subset of A° is selected, its application always leads to the choice of the most preferred act in the subset.

their knowledge may cause their *perceived* sets of possibilities to differ and consequently their rational behavior.

It is also clear that the relevant preference ordering or criterion is not independent of one's state of knowledge. For example, if the uncertainty of payoff values cannot be specified by cardinal probabilities, an ordering based upon expected payoff values cannot be used to determine the optimal act. Of course, the state of one's knowledge does not uniquely determine the criteria which can be applied to choice. If, for example, cardinal probabilities are assigned to payoffs, then besides expected payoff criteria, such criteria as the minimax and maximax can be applied.

J. Simon's Objections to "Orthodox" Decision Theory

Simon[59] objects to all of the previous decision-making theories (with the possible exception of Shackle's) upon the grounds that they imply that

(i) the individual is more rational than he actually is, and
(ii) that they require knowledge of him which is in excess of the human mind.

This, it is claimed, is not only true of traditional theories, such as those based upon expectations of gain or utility, but is also true of such criteria as Wald's since they require a knowledge of the outcomes for all possible acts and states of nature. "The capacity of the human mind for formulating and solving complex problems is very small compared with the size of the problems whose solution is required for objectively rational behavior in the real world—or even for a reasonable approximation to such rationality."[60]

Simon's objection seems to be applicable to those decision theories in which the individual is supposed to have sufficient

---

[59] H. A. Simon, (i) "A Behavioral Model of Rational Choice," *Quarterly Journal of Economics*, vol. 79 (1955), pp. 99–118; (ii) *Models of Man*, John Wiley and Sons, New York, 1957.
[60] Simon, *Models of Man*, p. 198.

information to calculate "the" set of objective outcomes and to discover all the alternative acts which are open to him. These theories assume that the individual by using his thought processes does discover the objective set of possible outcomes and all of his possible acts. As a description of reality, such theories appear unsound. The rational decision theory which was formulated at the beginning of this chapter makes more modest assumptions. The individual is not assumed to discover "the" objective set of possible outcomes or to know the set of all of his possible alternative acts. Nevertheless, one suspects that Simon would object to this modest rational decision theory. Some possible objections are the following:

(i) The theory assumes that the individual acts after considering the whole of his preference ordering. In practice, the individual may focus his attention upon only a small part of his ordering (for emotional reasons), and this may lead him to act irrationally as previously defined.

(ii) It assumes that the individual does have a consistent ordering over the possible outcomes. In fact, the individual may act without formulating that ordering. The ordering may neither be complete nor transitive.

Yet these objections are much less serious than they appear to be at first sight, since behavior may be rational even if the preference ordering of possibilities is neither transitive nor complete. Instead of interpreting the previous theory of rational behavior literally, we might take it that the individual acts *as if* the assumptions of the theory hold. On this view, the individual need not order his acts completely and transitively if he wishes to act rationally. The individual may, in some particular circumstances, focus his attention on some general properties of the ordering, and these properties may be sufficient to determine rational behavior. For example, the individual may know that all elements in the proper subset J of $A°$ are preferred to all elements in $A° - J$. Given this, then he need not order the elements of $A° - J$ completely, transitively, or at all in order to act rationally. A complete and transitive ordering of elements in J may more than suffice to determine the rational act. An individual who wishes to act rationally need not always scan and transitively order all the possibilities in detail, for sometimes a rational choice can be made using some *general* mathematical or other properties of the ordering. This less detailed knowledge may be more than sufficient for the purpose of ensuring rational choice. The theory of rational behavior which has been outlined represents an extremum problem. It will be perceived that most analytical mathematical techniques used to determine extrema eliminate the necessity of comparing all or a large number of possibilities in detail and rely upon general properties which lead us to concentrate upon particular qualities of the relationship under consideration in order to determine the extrema. So, also, general properties of orderings are sometimes sufficient to determine rational behavior. This much is probably obvious, but it needs to be emphasized since it shows that traditional decision theories can be interpreted so that they are consistent with "bounded" rationality.

Simon is critical of criteria which involve extrema, for he is of the opinion that most "ordinary" individuals cannot solve such problems. This is an empirical question, but it seems possible that a lot of people can consciously or subconsciously maximize variables. In accepting this view, one need not reject Simon's satisfier approach. In some circumstances, the satisfier model is probably a close description of actual behavior.

K. Simon's Satisfier Theory

According to Simon, the individual divides outcomes into those which are satisfactory and those which are unsatisfactory, depending on whether they meet his aspiration level or not. In attempting to attain his aspiration level, the individual at first considers a restricted subset of acts A° of the total class of possible acts A. If there is no act within the set A° which permits the individual to achieve his aspiration level then, depending upon his persistence, he may adjoin new acts (this will involve effort and cost), or he may reduce his aspiration level. Once the individual attains his aspiration level he is satisfied and does not wish to attain a minimum or maximum solution.

Simon's theory has consistency implications. Let B represent the set of acts in $A°$ which meet the individual's aspiration level. Then, if B is non-empty, it is inconsistent to select an act in $A° - B$. If B is empty, the theory merely asserts that the individual will search for new acts or lower his aspiration level. But the interaction between the perception of possibilities and the setting of aspiration levels is inadequately explained.

While Simon rejects maximization or minimization criteria, they are not inconsistent with a satisfier approach. As I have suggested elsewhere,[61] the firm may wish to maximize one variable subject to satisfactory levels being achieved in others. Such an approach differs from Simon's, for it supposes maximization or minimization to be important. Such maximization or minimization may take place for outcome values of a subset of all possible acts.

L. A Theory for Consistent but not Necessarily Rational Behavior

We can conceive of theories of behavior which are different from the one outlined at the beginning of this chapter but which, nevertheless, rely on some consistency postulates. For instance, a theory satisfying the following assumptions does:

(i) At any point of time, the individual knows of a set $A°$ of all the possible acts A open to him. $A° \subseteq A$.

(ii) The individual assigns to the ith act of the set $A°$ a set of variables. We represent this set by D_i and assume all such sets assigned to $A°$ to form a set D. The elements of the D_i are called decision variables and may include weights (probability) values. The D_i sets may

[61] Tisdell, *op. cit.* in fn. 46.

or may not accord with the $O°_i$ sets and may be obtained by operations on the $O°_i$ sets.[62]

(iii) To the set of decision variables, the individual applies a rule or criterion, e.g., a minimax, expected profit, or maximax rule, to select the set from all the D_i which satisfies this rule. Let us represent this set by D_h.

(iv) The individual adopts the act which corresponds to the D_i set satisfying this rule or criterion. He adopts act h.

An act adopted in accordance with this theory need not accord with the rational act as defined in the earlier theory; i.e., act h need not accord with the rational act k as previously defined. In special cases it will. This theory includes the previous theory of rational behavior as a special case.

By using the above theory, which is dependent upon "the" decision set of possibilities, we shall develop the formal conditions of production which must be satisfied if the firm's output decision is to be in accordance with some of the above criteria. In so doing, we must remember that the decision set of possibilities need not be identical with the set of possibilities $O°$ nor with "the" set of objective possibilities. Also criteria applied to D can result in acts which are security biased in one direction when referred to D and security biased in the opposite direction when referred to $O°$.

In suggesting the latter behavior model, I do not wish to imply that all behavior is in accord with this theory. It is likely

[62] A concrete example may help to make this clear. Suppose that for some act $\alpha_1 \in A°$, the individual believes that all possible profit values π from the adoption of this act fall in the range $1,000 \leq \pi \leq 3,000$. Now, for the purposes of decision-making, he may eliminate some of these values from consideration because, for example, they have such a low probability of occurrence. Profit values in the range $1,500 \leq \pi \leq 2,500$ may be assigned to α_1, and similar *restricted* payoffs may be assigned other acts. The assignments may diverge from what is felt to be possible. But, given these assigned values or decision values, the final choice is made acting in *consistency* with an ordering of them. For example, a rule such as the minimax might be applied to this restricted set or decision set in order to choose the "optimal" act.

(i) that decision sets are not always specified,

(ii) that the individual sometimes acts without a clearcut aim in mind,

(iii) that, if he has a clearcut aim and decision set, he sometimes makes mistakes in selecting his act.

The above rational and consistent types of behavior theory are in accord with the view that behavior is diverse and that aims differ from individual to individual and for the same individual in different circumstances. But behavior is even more diverse than may appear from these theories because individuals can act inconsistently with their aims.[63]

[63] It is also clear from the works of several economists, including those of G. Myrdal, that individuals' formulated aims can be inconsistent and confused.

CHAPTER III

Static Production Decisions

A. Introduction

The purposes of this chapter are several. It will outline the production implications, for the purely competitive firm, of various criteria if the firm acts under conditions of price uncertainty and in accordance with the previous theory of consistent behavior. It will show that, if a few general conditions are satisfied, some of the classical production theorems for perfect competition can be extended to cover production under uncertainty. This will be done by introducing a maximum equivalence proposition.

It will be assumed that the firm's decision set of price possibilities

    (i) contains more than one possible price, and
    (ii) is independent of the criterion used by the firm.

Assumption (i) is made in order to retain an essential element of price uncertainty, viz., that no one price appears certain. Assumption (ii) is made for notational convenience; it enables us to use the one set throughout the discussion, but it is not essential for a formal statement of conditions.

This chapter gives substance to the following statements:

    (i) Given the production model of this chapter, the firm's actual production can *always* be obtained as the production combination which maximizes an imputed profit function which is based upon a shadow vector.
    (ii) For some criteria, these shadow price vectors can be readily identified. The solution of the appropriate simulated maximization problem for any criterion is

identical to the production level arising from the criterion's consistent application. The shadow price vector of the simulated maximization problem is called "simple" if it is an element of the firm's decision set. The conversion of the solution of a criterion problem to the solution of a simulated maximization problem is called "simple" if a simple price vector occurs in the simulated problem.

The use of shadow prices effects a simplification (i) because it reduces some decision problems to readily identified maximization ones and (ii) because it enables us to treat differences in production as arising merely from differences in shadow prices (shadow price ratios). The shadow prices enable us to treat diverse behavior within a manageable framework.

Unless otherwise stated, it is assumed that price is the only variable which is subject to uncertainty. As far as the individual firm is concerned, price is assumed not to vary with its output, and also the individual firm is assumed to make static plans. Once static plans are acted upon, they are put into practice without revision. In some period $t - n$, $n > 0$, the firm plans to produce a specific quantity of output for period t, and begins to take steps to achieve this goal. If output is a controlled variable, then subsequently, and irrespective of what happens after $t - n$, the firm will produce the output in t which is planned in $t - n$. With dynamic decision-making, the plan is subject to revisions after operations have started.[1] The assumption of static decision-making drastically simplifies the theory of decision-making under uncertainty since it eliminates the possibility of variation of the controlled variables after a decision is made. While this assumption is retained for our first approximations, it is relaxed for later ones.

[1] The above distinctions between static and dynamic decision-making are made by Theil.

H. Theil: *Economic Forecasts and Policy*, North-Holland Publishing Company, 2nd revised edn.; Amsterdam, 1961, Chapter VII "Forecasts and Policy: Problems and Tools."

B. Assumptions

Before commencing detailed analysis, let us be specific about the assumptions. The following assumptions are made in relation to the individual firm's production:

(i) Prices are subject to uncertainty and the firm's decision .set of prices and probabilities can be taken as datum.

(ii) The production function is certain in $t - n$ for production relating to the output of t, $n > 0$.

(iii) The outputs for t and the inputs relating to the production of t must be decided prior to t in some period $t - n$.

(iv) The decision of $t - n$ is unalterable.

(v) The decision of $t - n$ is independent of other decisions, and the output of t is *solely* dependent upon the decision made in $t - n$.

(vi) The discount rate is zero. This assumption is made as a simplification, since interest rates are not essential to the theme of the analysis. Both inputs and outputs are controlled variables.[2]

Before beginning technical analysis, we ought to be familiar with some situations in which a decision of $t - n$ exactly determines the output possibilities of t. Putting legal and institutional factors temporarily to one side, let us concentrate upon physical relationships.

It is possible to conceive of a case in which the output of t is solely dependent upon the input of $t - n$—is independent of the inputs of other periods. In this case a unique lag between inputs and outputs occurs, and substitution is only possible in $t - n$. The time points at which substitution is possible can vary. In some industries the decisions will take place in all time intervals, but in other industries substitution is only possible at spaced intervals. For instance, in agriculture, decisions upon inputs may only be made during the planting season, which may occur at spaced intervals. In this theoretical example, it is the lack of substitutability of factors and products at times other than $t - n$ which dictates that

[2] H. Theil: *op. cit.*, pp. 373–374.

they be decided upon in $t - n$ and that the factors be applied in $t - n$ with a view to the resultant output.

However, this assumes that there are no lags in both hiring factors and in dispensing with them. In the absence of these lags, the prices of the factors which are hired and disposed of in $t - n$ will normally be certain. But frequently there are lags for institutional, technical, and administrative reasons. Because of these lags, input prices can be uncertain if a prior decision must be reached for the employment or disposal of factors at future market prices. Allowing for these employment and disposal lags, it might be more realistic to imagine a case in which the output of t is physically and solely dependent upon the inputs of $t - \theta$. The inputs of $t - \theta$ are decided in $t - n$ ($n > \theta$) because of the existence of a lag of $n - \theta$. In this case, factors and products of t are not substitutable after $t - n$.

There are other theoretical examples which accord with the above set of assumptions. For instance, the output of t may be dependent upon the inputs of several periods. Yet, if this is the case, all of these inputs must be decided in $t - n$. This could be done for a wide range of different reasons. Our requirement is that all of the values of the controlled variables which influence the output of t be decided in $t - n$.

C. A One Product Model

Before dealing with the general multi-commodity production problem, it may be best to introduce a simple one-product problem. The firm is assumed to produce one product, and the combination of factors which is required for that product is decided in $t - n$. Although all the factors may not be applied in $t - n$, our general assumptions require that their quantities and time of application be decided then. For this example only, factor prices are assumed to be certain.

The firm's decision problem can be considered as one of choosing an optimal level of output for t if factors are optimally combined by the decision of $t - n$. In making its decision of $t - n$, the firm will be uncertain of its product's price in t. In making this decision, we suppose that the firm acts upon some identifiable set of price possibilities. This decision set may or may not include all prices which the firm anticipates as possible for its product in t.[3]

In terms of some current language, each price of the firm's decision set represents a "possible" state of nature. Against these possible states of nature, the firm has a number of strategies. In this case, the firm's strategies are the levels of output which it can plan in $t - n$. The firm's strategies and the decision set of prices (states of nature) determine the outcomes, i.e., the "possible" profit values which are relevant for the firm's decision. Although the firm's actual profit outcome will depend upon its strategy and the prevailing state of nature, this outcome may not be included in the preceding set of *decision* possibilities.[4] *Despite* this, we shall refer to price and profit values of the decision set as possible values. This method of reference will be used until a different usage is specified.

Taking the decision set of possible prices for this one product case as datum, let us consider the optimal production levels for some different criteria. In this case, the set of possible product prices may consist of a finite or infinite number of price values, but these are assumed to be within finite bounds. Let p represent an element of this set. In addition, the firm has a set of possible levels of output of the product, and we will let x represent an element of this set. The set of possible product prices are those for the output (equals sales) of t, and the output possibilities are those which can be planned at $t - n$ for period t. If factor prices are known and if factors are always combined

---

[3] To make this clear, let $\P$ represent the firm's decision set of price possibilities and let Ω represent the set of prices which it believes to be subjectively possible. Then, the sets $\P$ and Ω may, but need not be, equal. Unless otherwise stated below, it will be assumed that $\P \subseteq \Omega$ and, hence, the price values in the decision set will be subjectively possible. It is, however, not essential to make this assumption, and the theorems below hold provided merely that the firm is prepared to act consistently on the basis of $\P$. Neither $\P$ nor Ω may be subset of the "objectively" possible set of prices.

[4] The decision set of price possibilities is not necessarily equivalent to "the" objective set of price possibilities.

to minimize the cost of any output, the possible levels of profit can be represented by the function

$$\phi = \phi(x, p) = px - C(x) \qquad 3.1$$

where the arguments x and p signify the possible levels of the product's output and price respectively and $C(x)$ represents total cost.

The problem is to determine the firm's optimal level of output for period t if this must be decided in period $t - n$ on the basis of $\phi(x, p)$. A solution only exists if the firm's aim is suitably specified for the problem. Assuming that there is more than one product price in the decision set (this is a reasonable assumption if price uncertainty exists), we notice immediately that the aim of profit maximization cannot be used to select "the" optimal level of output. If the marginal cost is not perfectly inelastic, different optimal values of output will attach to the different possible price values. In the ex-ante situation in $t - n$, there is nothing in the profit maximization criterion which enables an optimal output to be selected. Without going into details, let us consider the application of some other criteria to this decision problem.

(i) As generally used, the criterion of maximization of anticipated profit requires that the firm anticipate the occurrence of one particular price. If the marginal cost function is differentiable, output is optimal when the anticipated price equals marginal cost when marginal cost is increasing and average variable cost is covered. Yet this criterion is inadequate for application to conditions of uncertainty. Under uncertainty, the firm will generally anticipate more than one price as possible. If the firm does anticipate a number of price possibilities, the anticipated profit criterion does not enable us to predict the firm's action.[5]

[5] The decision set of price possibilities must contain only one possible product price, if this rule is to be applied. It may, for instance, just consist of the most probable price of the product.

(ii) If the firm adopts the Wald or maximin criterion, it wishes to assure itself of a gain no less than the maximum of the minimum gains for all acts. It should produce the level of output for which

$$\text{Max Min } \phi(x, p) \qquad 3.2$$
$$\quad x \quad p$$

occurs. In the matrix case in which the elements a_{ij} represent profit for the ith act when the jth state of nature prevails, the firm should select the output level which gives the maximum of the minimum profits in each row; i.e., it should select the output value corresponding to

$$\text{Max Min } a_{ij}. \qquad 3.3$$
$$\quad i \quad j$$

The Wald criterion, like those to be subsequently considered, is consistent with the fundamental condition for price uncertainty, i.e., with the possibility of more than one price.

(iii) If the firm adopts the maximax criterion, it aims to maximize its maximum possible level of profit. It should produce the output for

$$\text{Max Max } \phi(x, p). \qquad 3.4$$
$$\quad x \quad p$$

In the matrix case, the firm should select the output level which gives a maximum of the row maxima of profits, i.e., the output level for

$$\text{Max Max } a_{ij}.$$
$$\quad i \quad j$$

(iv) Both the Wald and the maximax criteria are special cases of the Hurwicz criterion. The firm adopting the Hurwicz criterion aims to maximize an index consisting of the weighted sum of the maximum and minimum possible profit for each output level. A fixed pessimism weight β is assigned to the lowest profit outcome for each level of profit and, an optimism weight $(1 - \beta)$ is assigned to the highest profit outcome for each output level. The firm wishes to maximize the index

$$\beta \operatorname*{Min}_{p} \phi(x, p) + (1 - \beta) \operatorname*{Max}_{p} \phi(x, p). \qquad 3.5$$

Its optimal level of output is the output value for

$$\operatorname*{Max}_{x} \{\beta \operatorname*{Min}_{p} \phi(x, p) + (1 - \beta) \operatorname*{Max}_{p} \phi(x, p)\}. \qquad 3.6$$

In the matrix case, the optimal level of output is the value in the rows for

$$\operatorname*{Max}_{i} \{\beta \operatorname*{Min}_{j} a_{ij} + (1 - \beta) \operatorname*{Max}_{j} a_{ij}\}. \qquad 3.7$$

When $\beta = 1$ the Hurwicz solution is the same as the Wald one, and when $\beta = 0$ it is the same as the maximax.

(v) If the firm adopts the Bayes criterion it wishes to produce an output which maximizes its expected profit. Showing mathematical expectation by E, the firm wishes to produce the output for

$$\operatorname*{Max}_{x} E[\phi(x, p)]. \qquad 3.8$$

But

$$\operatorname*{Max}_{x} E[\phi(x, p)] = \operatorname*{Max}_{x} \phi(x, E[p])$$
$$= \operatorname*{Max}_{x} \{E[p]x - C(x)\} \qquad 3.9$$

since the profit function is linear in p. If the cost function is differentiable, then expected profits will be at a maximum when

$$E(p) = C'(x),$$

$C''(x) > 0$, and average variable cost is increasing. For a maximum, production must be such that expected price is equal to marginal cost when marginal cost is increasing. In addition, a net surplus must be realized on current production.

In the previous example, the optimal conditions for the different criteria have not been stated in detail. We shall now consider an n-commodity model and state the solutions of some criteria in detail. In stating the solutions, one of our most important tasks will be to find the price vectors and problems which give equivalent maximum solutions.

D. Conversions to Maxima

There are many interesting and useful maximum equivalence theorems, and some of them will be used in this analysis. Therefore, let us outline a few of them.

It is known that a linear function defined on a compact convex set[6] reaches a maximum in a boundary point of the set and that every boundary point of a closed convex set lies on a supporting hyperplane of the set. It follows that if the firm's production possibilities form a compact convex set and if its production combination corresponds to a point on the boundary of the set, its actual production bundle is a member of *a set* of boundary points which maximize an imputed linear profit function subject to its production possibilities. The firm's production will be on a boundary point of the production set if it is unable to increase its output of any product without increasing the input or decreasing the output of any other commodity. But the above proposition is of very limited value since, merely supposing a compact convex production set, a large number of boundary points may maximize an appropriate imputed linear profit function, e.g., if the boundary of the set consists of facets or linear segments, and also, the supporting hyperplane at every boundary point of a closed convex set need not be unique; e.g., it will not be if the set has corner points.

However, if the production possibility set is assumed to be

---

[6] The terminology which is used in this section for the properties of sets is the same as that used by T. C. Koopmans and is "standard." See T. C. Koopmans, *Three Essays on the State of Economic Science*, McGraw-Hill, New York, 1957.

compact and *strictly*[7] convex, any production combination
on the boundary of the set can be *uniquely* determined by
maximizing an appropriate imputed (linear) profit function
subject to the production possibility set. Indeed, if we are only
given that the set of the firm's production possibilities is
convex, and if its production occurs in a strictly convex
boundary point, its actual production bundle can be uniquely
determined by maximizing an appropriate imputed profit
function subject to the set. Yet it remains true that the supporting hyperplane at such a boundary point may not be unique;
e.g., a corner point may arise. The price ratios in the appropriate imputed profit functions are not necessarily unique.
There is not a one-to-one correspondence between these ratios
and "actual" production bundles.

But if in addition to compactness and strict convexity, the
boundary of the production set is everywhere differentiable
and production is always such that it is impossible to increase
the output of any product without increasing the input or
decreasing the output of any other commodity, then there is
one-to-one correspondence between commodity combinations
satisfying these conditions and price ratios in the imputed
linear profit functions which yield them if they are maximized subject to the production possibility set. More generally,
if the production possibility set is compact and convex, this
one-to-one correspondence holds for any production combination satisfying all the following conditions:

    (i) The combination is such that it is impossible to increase
        the output of any one commodity without increasing
        the input or decreasing the output of any commodity.
   (ii) The set is strictly convex in the production point.
  (iii) The point is situated in a differentiable interval of
        the production set.

[7] A set is, in effect, a strictly convex set if it is convex and every point
on its boundary is an extreme point. Any straight line segment connecting
any two different points in the set is, except for its end-points, interior to
the set. See Koopmans *op. cit.*, p. 24.

Yet even more general maximum equivalence theorems hold, and some are outlined in the footnote below.[8] The nature of the above theorems can be made clearer by considering an example.

Suppose that the firm's production is always on a production function

$$f(x_1, x_2, \ldots, x_q) = 0$$

which is at least twice differentiable and also is on the boundary of the closed convex production set. The variables $\{x_1, x_2, \ldots, x_q\}$ represent quantities of the firm's q commodities. Let $X = [x_1, x_2, \ldots, x_q]$ and let $P = [p_1, p_2, \ldots, p_q]$ where the elements of this vector represent the prices attached to each of the respective commodities. Then, adopting the Hicksian convention of treating factors as negative products, a profit function can be expressed as

$$V = \sum_{r=1}^{q} p_r x_r = PX \qquad 3.10$$

where P is a row vector and X is a column vector. Assuming specific price values, the necessary conditions for a maximum of V subject to $f(X) = 0$ are

$$\left. \begin{aligned} p_r &= \lambda f_r, \qquad r = 1, \ldots, q \\ f(X) &= 0. \end{aligned} \right\} \qquad 3.11$$

---

[8] Some of the theorems stated or used above are set out in Koopman *op. cit.*, and S. Karlin, *Mathematical Methods and Theory in Games, Programming and Economics*, Addison–Wesley Publishing Company, Reading, 1959, Vol. I, Appendix B.

The following extensions are clear. Take any point in the boundary of a compact but not necessarily convex (production) set. If this point is also in the boundary of the convex hull of the set, it can be obtained by maximizing a suitable imputed (linear) profit function subject to the (production) set or its convex hull. If, *in addition*, the convex hull of the set is *strictly* convex in this boundary point, the production bundle which maximizes this function will be unique. If *furthermore*, the boundary point is contained in a differentiable range of the boundary, the set will have a unique supporting hyperplane at this point. Hence, the above theorems extend to non-convex sets.

where λ is a Lagrange multiplier. The necessary conditions can also be expressed as

$$\frac{p_1}{f_1} = \frac{p_2}{f_2} = \ldots = \frac{p_{q-1}}{f_{q-1}} = \frac{p_q}{f_q}.$$

The sufficient condition is that the change of profit should be negative for all variations of the commodity quantities which satisfy the production function. This, as is well known, is satisfied if d^2f is positive definite subject to $df = \sum_r f_r dx_r = 0$.

Consider any particular commodity vector satisfying $f(X) = 0$. Let us represent it as $X^* = [x_1{}^*, x_2{}^*, \ldots, x_q{}^*]$. The problem is to show that an imputed profit function exists which, when maximized subject to the set of production possibilities, yields X^*. Since the price values in the imputed profit function can be varied independently of one another, there is at least one combination of price values such that

$$\frac{p_1}{f_1(X^*)} = \frac{p_2}{f_2(X^*)} = \ldots = \frac{p_q}{f_q(X^*)}. \qquad 3.12$$

If $\hat{P} = [\hat{p}_1, \hat{p}_2, \ldots, \hat{p}_q]$ represents one vector of price values which satisfies this set of equations, then any scalar multiple of $\hat{P}$ satisfies them and no other price vectors satisfy them. The values

$$\frac{\zeta_1 p_1}{f_1(X^*)}, \frac{\zeta_2 p_2}{f_2(X^*)}, \ldots, \frac{\zeta_q p_q}{f_q(X^*)}$$

are only equal if $\zeta_1 = \zeta_2 = \ldots = \zeta_{q-1} = \zeta_q$. Consequently, under these conditions, there is *only one supporting hyperplane* in commodity space which contains X^*.

If an imputed profit function

$$V = \zeta \hat{P} X,$$

where ζ is an appropriate scalar, is maximized subject to

$$f(X) = 0,$$

the maximum occurs for $X = X^*$. If we assume that d^2f is positive definite, X^* is the only X value for which this maximum occurs, since the production function is strictly convex, and the constrained profit function is strictly concave.[9]

E. The Solutions and Some Simple
Shadow Prices in a Multi-Commodity Model

The purpose of this section is to state the multi-commodity optimal production behavior of the purely competitive firm for different criteria assuming that the firm operates under price uncertainty and that the previous static decision-making assumptions are satisfied. In addition, the section will give the maximum equivalent problem for some criteria and identify their shadow price vectors, particularly noting cases in which these are "simple." Let X represent any possible commodity vector of the firm. Where χ represents the firm's set of production possibilities which can be chosen for t in $t - n$, $X \in \chi$. Let P represent any vector of prices for X. In the problems below, P will generally be assumed to be an element of the firm's decision set of price values ¶. ¶ consists of the collection of the firm's decision set of price vectors, and the firm aims to act consistently using ¶ as a basis for its selection of an X value. The X value for period t is decided in some period $t - n$ $(n \geq 1)$ and in consistency with ¶. As previously pointed out in a footnote, ¶ may, but need not, coincide with the set of price vectors which the firm believes are subjectively possible. The possible level of profit is a function of the available input-output possibilities and is represented by

$$\phi = \phi(X, P) \qquad \qquad 3.13$$

Unless stated otherwise, the relation will be interpreted in a general way—discontinuities and restrictions can underlie it.

Our course is now the following one: Taking a decision set of price vectors ¶, we obtain the optimal commodity vectors for the Wald, maximax, Hurwicz, and Bayes criteria. Also, we specifically identify some price vectors which yield the Wald, maximax, Hurwicz, and Bayes commodity optima as the

[9] Cf. Karlin, op. cit., p. 405.

solution of a maximum problem. Let us concentrate on each criterion in turn.

The Wald solution. The optimal Wald solution is

$$\operatorname*{Max}_{X} \operatorname*{Min}_{P} \phi(X, P). \qquad 3.14$$

Suppose that an optimal Wald solution occurs for the commodity vector $X = X_0$ and the price vector $P = P_0$, i.e.,

$$\operatorname*{Max}_{X} \operatorname*{Min}_{P} \phi(X, P) = \phi(X_0, P_0). \qquad 3.15$$

Our aim is to find the condition for

$$\operatorname*{Max}_{X} \phi(X, P_0) = \operatorname*{Max}_{X} \operatorname*{Min}_{P} \phi(X, P). \qquad 3.16$$

An identical maximum solution involving P_0 need not occur for

$$\operatorname*{Max}_{X} \phi(X, P_0) \geq \phi(X_0, P_0). \qquad 3.17$$

If a saddle point exists for function ϕ at (X_0, P_0), then the equality of expression 3.16 will be satisfied and the maximum solution will be identical to the minimax one. Using the von Neumann–Morgenstern definition,[10] (X_0, P_0) is a *saddle point* of ϕ if at the same time $\phi(X, P_0)$ assumes its maximum at $X = X_0$ and $\phi(X_0, P)$ assumes its minimum at $P = P_0$. If a saddle point exists at (X_0, P_0),

$$\operatorname*{Max}_{X} \phi(X, P_0) = \operatorname*{Min}_{P} \phi(X_0, P). \qquad 3.18$$

But

$$\operatorname*{Min}_{P} \phi(X_0, P) = \phi(X_0, P_0) = \operatorname*{Max}_{X} \operatorname*{Min}_{P} \phi(X, P). \qquad 3.19$$

Hence, from equations 3.18 and 3.19, *the existence of a saddle point for ϕ at (X_0, P_0) ensures that the maximin solution can be replaced by an identical one found by maximizing ϕ*

[10] J. von Neumann and O. Morgenstern: *Theory of Games and Economic Behavior*, Princeton University Press, Princeton 1944.

(X, P_0) *with respect to* X. The prices of the price vector P_0 are treated as constants.

But going further than this—only if a saddle point exists at (X_0, P_0) can the maximin solution be converted to an equivalent maximum one of the specific form, $\underset{X}{\text{Max}}\, \phi(X, P_0)$. Proof: if a saddle point does not exist at (X_0, P_0), then $\phi(X_0, P_0)$ is not simultaneously the minimum of $\phi(X_0, P)$ and the maximum of $\phi(X, P_0)$. If $\phi(X_0, P_0)$ is the minimum of $\phi(X_0, P)$ then, if a saddle does not exist at (X_0, P_0), $\phi(X_0, P_0)$ is *not* the maximum of $\phi(X, P_0)$. If a saddle point does not exist at (X_0, P_0) then $\text{Max}\, \phi(X, P_0)$ occurs for some value other than X_0. This maximum point, say $\phi(X_\alpha, P_0)$, cannot be another saddle point value, for if a number of saddle points exist they have the same profit value.[11] In other words, if (X_α, P_0) and (X_0, P_0) are both saddle points

$$\phi(X_\alpha, P_0) = \phi(X_0, P_0) \qquad\qquad 3.20$$

and

$\underset{X}{\text{Max}}\, \phi(X, P_0)$ occurs for (X_α, P_0) and (X_0, P_0).

Consequently, if a saddle point does not exist at (X_0, P_0), then

$$\underset{X}{\text{Max}}\, \phi(X, P_0) = \phi(X_\alpha, P_0) > \phi(X_0, P_0). \qquad 3.21$$

Given the state P_0, the maximizing strategy X_α gives greater profit than does the firm's Wald strategy. But if (X_α, P_0) is not a saddle point, then obviously

$$\underset{P}{\text{Min}}\, \phi(X_\alpha, P) < \underset{P}{\text{Min}}\, \phi(X_0, P) \qquad\qquad 3.22$$

and the firm does not achieve its maximin strategy by producing X_α. *If a saddle point exists for the possible profit function $\phi(X, P)$, then, and only then, does the Wald solution convert to an identical maximization one based upon one of the possible states of nature.* Of course, even though the solution need not be

[11] *Ibid*, p. 95.

simple, the Wald solution will always convert to a maximization one if production possibilities form a compact convex set and production is in the boundary of the set.

As a particular instance of the existence of a saddle point, let us consider dominance. Where P' is one price vector and $\bar{P}'$ represents all other possible price vectors, the vector P' is dominant for the Wald solution if

$$\phi(X, P') < \phi(X, \bar{P}'). \qquad 3.23$$

It immediately follows that

$$\operatorname*{Min}_{P} \operatorname*{Max}_{X} \phi(X, P) = \operatorname*{Max}_{X} \phi(X, P'). \qquad 3.24$$

Also,

$$\operatorname*{Max}_{X} \operatorname*{Min}_{P} \phi(X, P) = \operatorname*{Max}_{X} \phi(X, P') \qquad 3.25$$

because

$$\operatorname*{Min}_{P} \phi(X, P) = \phi(X, P') \qquad 3.26$$

for any value of X.

Hence, given dominance,

$$\operatorname*{Min}_{P} \operatorname*{Max}_{X} \phi(X, P) = \operatorname*{Max}_{X} \operatorname*{Min}_{P} \phi(X, P), \qquad 3.27$$

which implies that a saddle point exists. *The dominance case is a special one in which a saddle point always exists.*

Let us consider a special dominance case. To divide the commodities into factors and products, let any quantity with a subscript in the set $\{1, 2, \ldots, m\}$ represent the quantity of an input, and let any quantity with a subscript in the set, $\{m + 1, m + 2, \ldots, q\}$ represent the quantity of a product. We shall show that if the highest possible price of each factor can occur along with the lowest price for each product, Wald dominance exists for the vector of highest factor and lowest product prices. The maximum equivalent solutions will also be stated for this case.

Let p_{r1} represent the lowest possible price of the rth commodity, and let p_{rn} represent its highest possible price, and suppose that the price vector $P_0 = [p_{1n}, p_{2n}, \ldots, p_{mn}; p_{m+1, 1},$

..., p_{q1}] is possible, i.e., a member of the decision set. Now, since a linear profit function is defined subject to the production possibilities,

$$\phi(X, P_0) < \phi(X, \bar{P}_0),$$

where $\bar{P}_0$ is any price vector other than P_0 in the decision set, and, hence, given our previous results,

$$\text{Max Min } \phi(X, P) = \text{Max } \phi(X, P_0).$$
$$\quad X \quad P \qquad\qquad\qquad X$$

To take a more specific instance, suppose that production is always on a twice differentiable production function $f(X) = 0$. Then, the Wald solution can be found by maximizing

$$V = P_0 X \qquad\qquad 3.28$$

subject to

$$f(X) = 0. \qquad\qquad 3.29$$

To find this maximum, we maximize

$$z = P_0 X - \lambda f(X)$$

where λ is a Lagrange multiplier. The necessary conditions for a maximum of this function are:

$$\left.\begin{array}{ll} p_{rn} = \lambda f_r & r = 1, \ldots, m \\ p_{r1} = \lambda f_r & r = m + 1, \ldots, q \\ f(X) = 0. & \end{array}\right\} \qquad 3.30$$

This gives $q + 1$ equations in $q + 1$ unknowns.

The sufficient condition for a maximum will be satisfied if $d^2 z$ is negative for all variations of output which satisfy the production function. Now,

$$d^2 z = -\lambda\, d^2 f \qquad\qquad 3.31$$

and

$$d^2 f = \sum_r \sum_s f_{rs}\, dx_r\, dx_s \qquad\qquad 3.32$$

where $s = 1, \ldots, q$.

Since $\lambda > 0$, d^2z will be negative definite if $d^2f > 0$ for all variations of output which satisfy the production function. Therefore, if d^2f is positive definite subject to

$$df = \sum_r f_r \, dx_r = 0, \qquad 3.33$$

d^2z will be negative definite subject to the variations set by the production function, and the sufficient conditions for a maximum will be satisfied. d^2f will be positive definite subject to the restriction of equation 3.33 if the following bordered principal minors of the production function and its bordered discriminant are all negative:

$$\begin{vmatrix} 0 & f_1 \\ f_1 & f_{11} \end{vmatrix} < 0, \begin{vmatrix} 0 & f_1 & f_2 \\ f_1 & f_{11} & f_{12} \\ f_2 & f_{21} & f_{22} \end{vmatrix} < 0, \ldots, \begin{vmatrix} 0 & f_s \\ f_r & f_{rs} \end{vmatrix} < 0 \qquad 3.34$$

where $r, s = 1, \ldots, q$.

Denoting any two commodities by the subscripts r and s, the marginal conditions of 3.30 imply that

$$-\frac{dx_s}{dx_r} = \frac{f_r}{f_s} = \frac{p_{r0}}{p_{s0}} \qquad 3.35$$

if the elements of P_0 are now indicated by p_{r0}. *In this dominance case*, the marginal requirements for a Wald optimum are that

 (i) the ratio of the lowest possible prices for any two products ($r > m$ and $s > m$) be equal to the (marginal) rate of substitution between the products in production;
 (ii) the ratio of the highest prices for any two factors ($r \leq m$ and $s \leq m$) be equal to their (marginal) technical rate of substitution;
 (iii) the ratio between the highest price for any factor ($r \leq m$) and the lowest price for any product ($s > m$) be equal to the (marginal) technical rate of transformation between the factor and the product.

Now, if d^2f is positive definite everywhere, this implies that the production function is *strictly* convex and that the constrained profit function is strictly concave.[12] In consequence, the profit function has at most one local maximum and any local maximum or extremum is an absolute maximum.[13]

But $d^2 f$ may, in fact, not be positive definite for all X values, and the profit function may not achieve a local maximum for any available X value. In such circumstances, a corner point solution may be optimal. For profit to be at a maximum, each product or group of products produced must yield a surplus, so that it does not pay to abandon the production of any product or group of products.

The case in which $P_0 = [p_{1n}, \ldots, p_{mn}; p_{m+1,1}, \ldots, p_{q1}]$ can occur has been pursued at length because the above conditions and procedures apply with minor modification to other Wald situations. Similar marginal, second-order, and absolute value conditions apply *mutatis mutandis* to any Wald solution which can be converted into a maximum one. This is so, provided that the production function satisfies the differentiability requirements. In dominance and non-dominance cases where a saddle point exists, the first-order conditions may be based upon a set of prices which contain some values each of which is not the highest possible for a factor, or the lowest possible price of a product.

If, as assumed previously, the firm produces only one good and this is subject to price uncertainty and if its costs are certain, this is a *dominance case* in which the highest possible price of the factors can occur along with the lowest possible price for the product. We have deduced that the Wald solution always converts to a simple maximum one in this case. Therefore, if p_1 is the lowest possible price for the product and if the cost function is at least twice differentiable, then the Wald optimum occurs for

$$p_1 = C'(x)$$

provided that $C''(x) > 0$ and average variable cost is increasing at this output level.

[12] For definitions of convexity, strict convexity, etc., of functions, see Karlin, *op. cit.*, pp. 404–405.
[13] Cf. Karlin, *op. cit.*, p. 405.

To conclude: If a saddle point exists and profit is maximized upon the basis of the price vector which corresponds to the saddle point, then the firm attains its maximin solution. Only if a saddle point exists can a maximin solution be attained by maximizing upon the basis of *one of the possible states of nature*. A saddle point exists if dominance is possible. If the highest possible price of factors can occur along with the lowest possible price for products, we have a special but nevertheless relevant case of dominance. In this case the maximin solution can be attained by maximizing profit upon the basis of the price vector of the highest possible price for factors and the lowest possible prices for products. Naturally, if the price of any commodity is certain, its lowest and highest possible price coincide.

The Maximax Solution. Where $\phi(X, P)$ represents the profit possibilities of the firm, let the firm's optimal maximax solution be

$$\underset{X}{\text{Max}} \, \underset{P}{\text{Max}} \, \phi = \phi(X_1, P_1). \qquad 3.36$$

It can be shown that

$$\underset{X}{\text{Max}} \, \underset{P}{\text{Max}} \, \phi(X, P) = \underset{X}{\text{Max}} \, \phi(X, P_1). \qquad 3.37$$

Any two maximax values commute since any two have the same characteristic property of being a maximum of $\phi(X, P)$. Commutativity implies that

$$\underset{X}{\text{Max}} \, \underset{P}{\text{Max}} \, \phi(X, P) = \underset{P}{\text{Max}} \, \underset{X}{\text{Max}} \, \phi(X, P).$$

The values (X_1, P_1) yield an absolute maximum of the function[14] $\phi(X, P)$. It follows that

$$\underset{P}{\text{Max}} \, \underset{X}{\text{Max}} \, \phi(X, P) = \underset{P}{\text{Max}} \, \phi(X_1, P) = \phi(X_1, P_1) \qquad 3.38$$

and that

$$\underset{X}{\text{Max}} \, \underset{P}{\text{Max}} \, \phi(X, P) = \underset{X}{\text{Max}} \, \phi(X, P_1) = \phi(X_1, P_1). \qquad 3.39$$

[14] For further discussion of commutativity see von Neumann and Morgenstern, *op. cit.*, pp. 91–93. They deal with other cases besides the maximax.

Expression 3.38, when taken in conjunction with the commutativity property and expression 3.39, implies that every maximax production decision has a *simple* maximum equivalent, i.e., an equivalent in which a maximax production combination can be found by maximizing an imputed profit function which is based upon *one of the possible* price vectors.

If the lowest possible price of each factor can occur simultaneously with the highest possible price for each product, then the optimal maximax solution occurs for

$$\text{Max } \phi(X, P_1)$$
$$\phantom{\text{Max }}_X$$

where

$$P_1 = [p_{11}, p_{21}, \ldots, p_{m1}; p_{m+1,n}, \ldots, p_{qn}].$$

The "state of nature" P_1 is dominant here since, for any combination of commodities, profits are highest for the occurrence of the vector P_1.

If, as before, production is always on the production function $f(X) = 0$, the maximax solution can be obtained by maximizing

$$V = P_1 X \qquad\qquad 3.40$$

subject to

$$f(X) = 0. \qquad\qquad 3.41$$

If the conditions of the last paragraph hold and if $f(X)$ is differentiable, the following are some necessary conditions for this maximum:

(i) The ratio of the highest possible prices for any two products must equal the technical rate of substitution between the products.

(ii) The ratio of the lowest possible prices for any two factors must be equal to the technical rate of substitution of the factors.

(iii) The ratio between the lowest price for any factor and the highest price for any product must be equal to the technical rate of transformation between the factor and the product.

To determine whether any output which satisfies the necessary conditions is a maximum, we must once again consider the second-order conditions and check corner-point values. If the vector $P_1 = [p_{11}, \ldots, p_{m+1,n}, \ldots, p_{qn}]$ is not in the decision set, a simple maximax solution still exists.

If the firm produces one product and costs are certain, dominance occurs for the maximax solution. Hence, if p_n represents the highest possible price for the product, then the maximax solution can be found by maximizing $p_n x - C(x)$. If this function is at least twice differentiable, the maximax optimum occurs for an output satisfying

$$p_n = C'(x)$$

if $C''(x) > 0$ and average variable cost is increasing at this output level.

Unlike the minimax solution, the maximax solution always converts into a simple and equivalent maximum solution in which one of the possible states of nature is treated as though it is certain. The Hurwicz solution does not always have a simple maximum equivalent.

The Hurwicz Solution. Let the Hurwicz solution be

$$\text{Max} \{\beta \underset{P}{\text{Min}} \, \phi(X, P) + (1 - \beta) \underset{P}{\text{Max}} \, \phi(X, P)\}$$
$$= \beta\phi(X^*, P_0) + (1 - \beta)\phi(X^*, P_1). \qquad 3.42$$

Then,

$$\underset{x}{\text{Max}} \{\beta\phi(X, P_0) + (1 - \beta)\phi(X, P_1)\}$$
$$\geq \beta\phi(X^*, P_0) + (1 - \beta)\phi(X^*, P_1). \qquad 3.43$$

But if dominance arises, the Hurwicz solution can be converted to a maximum one such that

$$\underset{x}{\text{Max}} \{\beta\phi(X, P_0) + (1 - \beta)\phi(X, P_1)\}$$
$$= \beta\phi(X^*, P_0) + (1 - \beta)\phi(X^*, P_1). \qquad 3.44$$

If

$$\left.\begin{array}{c} \phi(X, P_0) \leq \phi(X, P) \\ \\ \phi(X, P_1) \geq \phi(X, P) \end{array}\right\} \qquad 3.45$$

and

then "Hurwicz" dominance occurs. Given relationship 3.45,

$$\operatorname*{Min}_{P} \phi(X, P) = \phi(X, P_0) \qquad 3.46$$

and

$$\operatorname*{Max}_{P} \phi(X, P) = \phi(X, P_1). \qquad 3.47$$

Therefore

$$\operatorname*{Max}_{X} \{\beta \operatorname*{Min}_{P} \phi(X, P) + (1 - \beta) \operatorname*{Max}_{P} \phi(X, P)\}$$

$$= \operatorname*{Max}_{X} \{\beta\phi(X, P_0) + (1 - \beta)\phi(X, P_1)\}$$

$$= \beta\phi(X^*, P_0) + (1 - \beta)\phi(X^*, P_1). \qquad 3.48$$

As a particular case of "Hurwicz" dominance, suppose the vectors

$$P_1 = [p_{1n}, p_{2n}, \ldots, p_{mn}; p_{m+1,1}, \ldots, p_{q1}]$$

and

$$P_n = [p_{11}, p_{21}, \ldots, p_{m1}; p_{m+1,n}, \ldots, p_{qn}]$$

to be possible. Then, if production is on a production function $f(X) = 0$, the Hurwicz solution can be found by maximizing

$$\sum_{r=1}^{m} (\beta p_{rn} + (1 - \beta)p_{r1})x_r + \sum_{r=m+1}^{q} (\beta p_{r1} + (1 - \beta)p_{rn})x_r$$

$$3.49$$

subject to the production function. If the differentiability conditions are satisfied, the marginal conditions involve the price "indices" $\beta p_{rn} + (1 - \beta)p_{r1}$ for $r \leq m$ and $\beta p_{r1} + (1 - \beta)p_{rn}$ for $r \geq m + 1$. When $\beta = 0$ these first-order conditions are the same as those for the Wald criterion, and when $\beta = 1$ they are the same as for the maximax. As before, second-order conditions and boundary requirements must be met.

"Hurwicz dominance" always occurs in the one-product case if costs are certain. We know, from the above theorem, that the Hurwicz output can be obtained by maximizing $[\beta p_1 + (1 - \beta)p_n]x - C(x)$. If this function is at least twice differentiable, then a Hurwicz optimum occurs if

$$C'(x) = \beta p_1 + (1 - \beta)p_n,$$

$$C''(x) > 0$$

and if the average variable cost is increasing at the point of the equality.

The Bayes Solution. The Bayes solution occurs for

$$\text{Max } E[\phi(X, P)].$$
$$x$$

If $E(P) = [E(p_1), E(P_2), \ldots, E(p_q)]$ is a vector consisting of the expected prices of the q commodities, and if the set of production possibilities is compact and convex, then, due to the linearity of the unconstrained profit function, the Bayes solution can be obtained by maximizing

$$V = E(P)X = \sum_{r=1}^{q} E(p_r)x_r \qquad 3.50$$

subject to the production set. If production is always on a suitable differentiable function $f(X) = 0$, the first-order conditions for a maximum will be in terms of expected prices and rates of technical transformation and will be similar to the ones for the perfectly competitive firm. Similar second-order and boundary conditions will also be relevant.

It will be recalled that all of the previous analysis is based upon the assumption of an identifiable decision set. In postulating this decision set, we did not postulate its relation to actual prices nor to objectively possible prices. Neither did we postulate any special relationship between actual output and the optimal output under certainty, nor between maximum equivalent prices under uncertainty and actual prices. Obviously, the firm's output under uncertainty is the joint result of its predictions and criterion, and from the point of view of its actual profit both factors have an influence.

From the point of view of comparing profit under uncertainty with that under certainty, both the firm's criterion *and* the quality of its prediction are important. When we come to consider the firm's actual average profit in later chapters, we must take account of both factors.

CHAPTER IV

Static Plans and Dissimilar
Production Combinations

A. Introduction

Given the same production possibility set, production combinations can be different

(i) because criteria differ,
(ii) because decision sets differ, or
(iii) because various forms of inconsistent, non-rational or random (but not necessarily irrational) behavior arise.

If the firm makes static plans of the type outlined in the last chapter, dissimilar levels of production can be compared by utilizing maximum equivalence formulations. These dissimilarities of production can be treated, under various circumstances, as if they arise from a variation of the price parameters in the problem where an imputed (linear) profit function is to be maximized subject to the production possibility set. As under conditions of certainty, comparisons of production under conditions of uncertainty can be reduced to comparisons of constrained "profit" maxima. For a wide range of conditions, each production value can be conceived of as a value which maximizes an imputed profit function, and dissimilarities of production (or comparative static changes of production) can be viewed as stemming from variations in the shadow prices when the imputed profit function is maximized subject to the production set.

By adopting this maximum equivalence approach, it is possible to reinterpret many of the mathematical theorems which Hicks introduces for the perfect competition model so that they apply to production under price uncertainty. While there is mathematical similarity between the production theorems for price uncertainty and some of those for perfect competition, they differ in their economic interpretation and generality. Interestingly enough, theories which are applicable to production under uncertainty can mostly treat certainty as a special case, and in this respect they lead to increased generality.

In this chapter, we shall state a few of Hicks' production theorems and then, assuming consistent behavior, show their relevance, under conditions of price uncertainty, to the effect upon production of

(i) a change of criterion when the decision set is given; and

(ii) a change of the decision set when the criterion is given.

Consequently, we shall be able to compare the divergent effect upon production of different criteria and decision sets. In making these comparisons, we should not lose sight of the general idea that, under a large variety of conditions, the divergencies in production levels can be treated as arising from a change in the shadow price vector of an imputed profit maximization problem.

B. Some Preliminary General Observations
on Comparisons by
Maximum Equivalence

Before considering Hicks' particular assumptions, it may be helpful to make some general observations upon comparison of production levels via price parameter changes in a maximization model.

If a set χ is strictly convex and compact, each boundary point of the set is contained in *at least* one supporting hyperplane, and no two points on its boundary have a common supporting hyperplane. Take any two distinct points X_0 and X_1 in the boundary of the set and let $\mathscr{J}_0$ represent the set of supporting hyperplanes at X_0 and $\mathscr{J}_1$ represent those at X_1. Then, $\mathscr{J}_0 \cap \mathscr{J}_1$ is empty and the imputed linear functions which if maximized subject to the set χ yield X_0 differ from all of those which yield X_1. In our case, if the production possibility set is strictly convex and compact, and if production is always such that no product's output can be increased without increasing the input or decreasing the output of any other commodity,[1] then, taking any two production combinations X_0 and X_1 which satisfy these conditions, the shadow price vectors (and the shadow price ratio vectors) of the imputed profit maximization problems which yields X_0 are all different from those for the problems which yield X_1. If these production conditions are satisfied, every variation of production can be treated as arising from a change of shadow prices in a problem in which an imputed profit function is maximized subject to the set of production possibilities.

This relationship can be generalized further. If

   (i) production is always confined to merely a compact set χ;
  (ii) is always such that it is impossible to increase the output of any commodity without increasing the input or decreasing the output of another;
 (iii) is confined to points which are strictly convex in the convex hull $[\chi]$ of the production set;

then any variation from one production combination to another can be treated as arising from a change in the shadow prices of the appropriate imputed maximization problem. If, in addition to the fulfilment of these three conditions, production always falls in a differentiable segment of $[\chi]$, there is a unique supporting hyperplane for each such production combination, and there is a one-to-one correspondence between the production combinations which satisfy these conditions and the price ratio vectors of their appropriate imputed profit maximization problems.

It is clear that under very general conditions dissimilarities of production can be treated as if they arise from a variation of price parameters in a problem where an imputed (linear)

---

[1] It ought to be noted that this condition not only restricts production to points upon the boundary but to particular boundary points.

profit function is maximized subject to the production possibility set. It is reemphasised that in imputing the maximization problem, we do not imply that the firm actually determines its output by some maximization process. Rather than develop the argument on maximum equivalence and its relevance to dissimilarities of production in a very general way, it may be of more interest to the reader to see the specific way in which the theory can be linked to Hicks' analysis.

C. The Production Effects of Price Vector
Variations in a Constrained Maximum Problem

Before considering in detail dissimilarities in production combinations which arise under conditions of price uncertainty, we can profitably re-familiarize ourselves with the effects upon production of a variation in a price vector of a linear net profit function which is maximized subject to a differentiable production function. To be more specific, we should re-familiarize ourselves with the effect upon production of a change in the price vector P if

$$V = \sum_{r=1}^{q} p_r x_r = PX$$

is maximized subject to the production function

$$f(X) = 0,$$

which is assumed to be at least twice differentiable. Mathematically, the problem is identical to the Hicksian perfect competition one of finding the effect upon production of a change in a certain price vector when profit is constrained by the preceding production function.

For the price vector $[p_1, p_2, \ldots, p_q]$, the firm's constrained profit function is

$$z = \sum_{r=1}^{q} p_r x_r - \lambda f(x_1, x_2, \ldots, x_q)$$

where λ is the Lagrange multiplier. The necessary conditions for a maximum of this function are

$$p_r = \lambda f_r \qquad (r = 1, \ldots, q)$$

and

$$\frac{\partial z}{\partial \lambda} = f(x_1, x_2, \ldots, x_q) = 0.$$

4.1

If the price vector $[p_1, p_2, \ldots, p_q]$ changes, our assumptions imply that the firm will respond by altering its combination of resources in such a way that the marginal conditions continue to be satisfied. Therefore, the problem is to discover the change in production when prices change and the marginal conditions of expression 4.1 continue to be met. To obtain this change we differentiate the marginal conditions totally and obtain

$$dp_r - \lambda \sum_{s=1}^{q} f_{rs} \, dx_s - f_r \, d\lambda = 0 \qquad (r = 1, \ldots, q)$$

and

$$\sum_{s=1}^{q} f_s \, dx_s = 0.$$

4.2

Rearranging,

$$f_r d\lambda + \lambda \sum_{s=1}^{q} f_{rs} \, dx_s = dp_r \qquad (r = 1, \ldots, q)$$

and

$$\sum_{s=1}^{q} f_s \, dx_s = 0.$$

4.3

Equations 4.3 expressed differently are

$$0d\lambda + f_1 \, dx_1 + f_2 \, dx_2 + \ldots + f_q \, dx_q = 0$$

$$f_1 \, d\lambda + \lambda[f_{11} \, dx_1 + f_{12} \, dx_2 + \ldots + f_{1q} \, dx_q] = dp_1$$

$$\cdot$$
$$\cdot$$
$$\cdot$$

$$f_q \, d\lambda + \lambda[f_{q1} \, dx_1 + f_{q2} \, dx_2 + \ldots + f_{qq} \, dx_q] = dp_q$$

or

$$\begin{bmatrix} 0 & f_s \\ f_r & \lambda f_{rs} \end{bmatrix} \begin{bmatrix} d\lambda \\ dx_r \end{bmatrix} = \begin{bmatrix} 0 \\ dp_r \end{bmatrix} \qquad 4.4$$

where $r, s = 1, \ldots, q$.

Let

$$G = \begin{vmatrix} 0 & f_s \\ f_r & \lambda f_{rs} \end{vmatrix} = |g_{ij}| \qquad 4.5$$

where $r, s = 1, \ldots, q$ and $i, j = 1, \ldots, q + 1$. Then, by Cramer's Rule,

$$dx_s = \frac{\sum\limits_{r=1}^{q} dp_r G_{rs}}{G} \qquad 4.6$$

where $s = 1, \ldots, q$ and G_{rs} is the cofactor of element g_{ij} $= g_{r+1, \, s+1}$ in the matrix, $[g_{ij}]$. If

$$F = \begin{vmatrix} 0 & f_s \\ f_r & f_{rs} \end{vmatrix} \qquad 4.7$$

and if F_{rs} represents the cofactor of f_{rs}, then equation 4.6 reduces to

$$dx_s = \frac{\sum\limits_{r=1}^{q} F_{rs} \, dp_r}{\lambda F}. \qquad 4.8$$

The change in the output (or input) of the commodity s is found by summing the "technological" cofactors F_{rs} for the r commodities and then dividing by the determinant F times the scalar multiple λ.

In the absence of special knowledge, it is impossible to place a sign upon equation 4.8. However, if the price of the rth resource alone increases, then, if it is a product its supply increases and if it is a factor its input decreases. This can be shown as follows: Let $dp_r = 0$ for all $r \neq s$ and $dp_r > 0$ for $r = s$. Then,

$$dx_s = \frac{\sum\limits_{r=1}^{q} F_{rs} \, dp_r}{\lambda F} = \frac{F_{rr} \, dp_r}{\lambda F}. \qquad 4.9$$

Therefore,

$$\frac{\partial x_r}{\partial p_r} = \frac{F_{rr}}{\lambda F}. \qquad 4.10$$

Since $r + r$ is even then $(r + 1) + (r + 1)$ is even and F_{rr} is equal to the minor of f_{rr} with a positive sign attached. If the sufficient conditions, 3.34, for a maximum of profit are met, the minor of the qth commodity Δ_{qq} must be negative. Since the second last matrix in 3.34 is negative and since *any* commodity can occupy the $(1 + q)$th place in the bordered discriminant of the production function, the minor of the rth commodity Δ_{rr} must be negative. Hence, the cofactor of the rth commodity $F_{rr} = +(\Delta_{rr})$ is negative if the sufficient conditions for a maximum of profit are met. Also the sufficient conditions, 3.34, for a maximum imply that the bordered discriminant F is negative. Therefore,

$$\frac{\partial x_r}{\partial p_r} = \frac{F_{rr}}{\lambda F} > 0 \qquad 4.11$$

because $\lambda > 0$. For $m + 1 \leq r \leq q$, $\partial x_r / \partial p_r > 0$, and, since factors are treated as negative products, the change in the input of a factor whose price alone rises is of opposite sign.

The effect upon the input and output of all commodities of a rise in the price of a single commodity r, all other prices remaining unchanged, is

$$dx_s = \frac{F_{rs}}{\lambda F} \, dp_r. \qquad (s = 1, \ldots, q) \qquad 4.12$$

From the previous argument it is known that $dx_r > 0$, but the effect upon the input or output of the other commodities is unknown. Only if all the cofactors F_{sr}, where $s = 1, \ldots, m$ are positive and, if the cofactors F_{sr}, $s = m + 1, \ldots, q$, are negative will an increase in the price of product r lead to an increase in the employment of all factors and to an increase in the output of all products. In this case, complementarity is dominant both on the product and factor side.[2] Complementarity dominates if constant returns to scale exist,[3] but, with decreasing returns, substitute and regressive relations become more important.

Let us now consider the effect of a rise in the price of a *group* of products. For simplicity suppose that all product prices increase.[4] Then the change in the output or input of commodity s is

$$\mathrm{d}x_s = \sum_{r=m+1}^{q} \frac{F_{rs}\,\mathrm{d}p_r}{\lambda F}, \qquad\qquad 4.13$$

where $s = 1, \ldots, q$.

Unless all of the cofactors $F_{rs} > 0$ for $r \leq m$ and all of the cofactors $F_{rs} < 0$ for $r = m + 1, \ldots, q$, a rise in the price of one or more products can lead to a decrease in the output or input of some commodities. If the relative frequency of positive product cofactors is low, then there is a low probability of a rise in the price of any product causing a decline in the output of any other randomly chosen product. However, in the absence of further knowledge, the effect upon the output of any particular product is unknown. Similar conclusions hold for factor relations.

Comparisons of optimal aggregate output are complicated by the existence of substitute or regressive relations. A rise in the price of one or more products and a fall in the price of one or more inputs can lead to an increase in the output of some products and to a decrease in the output of others. In consequence, comparison of aggregate output involves an index problem, which can only be avoided in special instances.

[2] Hicks, *Value and Capital*, 2nd edn., Clarendon Press, Oxford, 1946, pp. 97–98.

[3] Hicks, *op. cit.*, pp. 94–95 and pp. 322–323.

[4] If the prices of all products do not increase, then we merely put $\mathrm{d}p_r = 0$ in expression 4.13 for those products showing no rise and the following statements apply *mutatis mutandis*.

Having considered some theorems for a change of a constrained maximum, we shall now apply them in two different ways. First, we shall apply them to the effects upon production of a change in the set of decision prices when the firm's criterion remains unchanged. Secondly, we shall apply them to the effects upon production of a change in criterion when the decision set remains unchanged. For the purposes of this analysis, the assumptions of the previous chapter will be assumed to hold. This means that the foregoing analysis applies to conditions of static decision-making.

D. The Effect Upon Production
of a Variation of the Decision Price Set

Consider two different price decision sets ¶ and ¶' and let P represent any price vector in ¶ and P' represent any price vector in ¶'. Beginning with the minimax criterion, let us compare the optimal minimax production levels for both decision sets. Suppose that saddle points exist for (X_0, P_0) and (X'_0, P'_0). Then for the first decision set ¶,

$$\text{Max}_X \text{Min}_P \phi(X, P) = \phi(X_0, P_0) = \text{Max}_X \phi(X, P_0)$$

and for the second decision set ¶',

$$\text{Max}_X \text{Min}_P \phi(X, P') = \phi(X'_0, P'_0) = \text{Max}_X \phi(X, P'_0).$$

To compare the two optimal levels of output X and X'_0, we make use of maximum equivalence. The difference in these two optimal output levels is equivalent to the change in production when profit is first maximized upon the price vector P_0 and then upon the vector P'_0.

Given that the production function is at least twice differentiable and satisfies conditions 3.34, the previous "Hicksian" maximization theorems can be applied. If the minimax price vector P'_0 contains one product price which exceeds its corresponding value in the vector P_0 then, other vector prices remaining constant, the output of the higher priced product will increase. Similarly, if the vector P'_0 contains one factor price which is lower than its corresponding value in P_0, then a change to decision set P' will increase the employment of the lower "priced" factor if all other imputed prices remain unchanged. If the vector P'_0 is a scalar multiple of P, optimal production will be the same for both decision sets. The change in the input or output of each commodity for a change in the minimax price vector can be found by extending equation 4.13. Where the change of the price vector is finite, the relevant partial derivatives which form the basis for this equation must be evaluated at an intermediate point so as to accord with the mean value theorem.[5] There is no need to state this result specifically because the qualitative conditions of equation 4.13 carry over to the finite case since we have assumed the required monotonicity condition. If $P'_0 > P_0$ because one or more product prices are higher in P'_0, the effect upon the employment of factors and the output of products will depend upon whether complementarity is dominant. The effect upon aggregate production of a change in the minimax price vector from P_0 to P'_0 (where $P'_0 > P_0$) is not predictable in the absence of further information.

If the firm adopts other criteria, such as the Bayes or maximax criterion, then, by taking the relevant maximization price vectors, we can once more apply the preceding theorems *mutatis mutandis*. Since the application is obvious, there is no need to give an account of it.

Index problems arise in the comparison of production in the multi-product case. However, they do not arise in the one-product case if factor prices are certain. In this one-product case, the minimax solution always converts to a simple maximum one. For the minimax criterion, any rise in the product's least possible price will cause optimal output to increase if average variable costs are covered and marginal cost is not perfectly inelastic. Under the same production conditions,

---

[5] P. A. Samuelson, *Foundations of Economic Analysis*, Harvard University Press, Cambridge, 1947, pp. 46–52. For an introductory mathematical survey of theorems of the mean: R. Courant, *Differential and Integral Calculus*, Vol. I, Interscience Publishers, New York, 1937, pp. 102–106.

output will expand for the Bayes criterion and the maximax criterion if the expected price and the greatest possible price respectively increase. Insofar as uncertainty output solutions convert to maximum ones, the supply function for a change in the imputed price component is identical *in form* to the supply function under certainty.

E. The Effect Upon Production
of Different Criterion

We turn now to the second comparative problem: the comparison of optimal levels of output for different criterion when the decision set of prices ¶ remains constant. Let a saddle point exist for (X_0, P_0). Then, the minimax solution is

$$\text{Max Min } \phi(X, P) = \phi(X_0, P_0) = \text{Max } \phi(X, P_0).$$
$$\quad X \quad P \qquad\qquad\qquad\qquad\qquad\qquad X$$

Also, suppose the Bayes solution to be

$$\text{Max } \phi(E[P], X) = \phi(E[P], X_E),$$
$$\quad X$$

and the maximax solution to be

$$\text{Max Max } \phi(X, P) = \phi(X_1, P_1) = \text{Max } \phi(X, P_1).$$
$$\quad X \quad P \qquad\qquad\qquad\qquad\qquad\qquad X$$

Our problem is to determine the relationship among the commodity vectors X_0, X_E, and X_1. This will depend upon the relationship among P_0, $E[P]$, and P_1. If factor prices are certain and if product prices are uncertain, and if the lowest price of any product can occur along with the lowest price of every other, and if the highest price of all products can occur simultaneously, then the vector relationships are $P_0 < E[P] < P_1$. If the price for one product only is highest in the vector P_1, lower in the vector $E(P)$ and lowest in the vector P_0, the optimal output of that product will be highest for the maximax criterion, lower for the Bayes criterion, and lowest for the Wald criterion. This follows at once from the discussion of equation 4.10 if the production function satisfies the relevant conditions. However, this result does not indicate the effect of the change upon aggregate output. Only if complementarity is dominant will the maximax, Bayes, and Wald criteria lead to aggregate product outputs which are of descending magnitude if $P_0 < E[P] < P_1$. For the multi-good firm, the output of products will not necessarily be greatest for the maximax criterion, next highest for the Bayes criterion, and least for the Wald criterion, because the output of some products will increase and the output of others will decrease if substitutability is important. Similarly, the aggregate employment of factors need not be least for the Wald criterion, higher for the Bayes criterion, and highest for the maximax. But these ambiguities of comparison only arise in the multi-product case.

If the price of the output of a one-product firm is uncertain and if its costs are certain, the firm's output will be highest for the maximax criterion, lower for the Bayes criterion, and lowest for the Wald criterion. This will be so, provided that marginal cost is not perfectly inelastic and average variable cost is covered. To compare the Wald, Bayes and maximax level of optimal output in this simple case, let $\{p_1, p_2, \ldots, p_n\}$ be the product decision set of prices and suppose that $p_n > p_{n-1} > \ldots > p_1$. The firm has a profit function

$$\Pi = px - C(x)$$

and a supply function

$$x = g(p),$$

where $g(p)$ is the inverse of the function $p = C'(x)$ and $[C(x)/x]' \geq 0$. By the inverse rule of differentiation,

$$g'(p) = \frac{dx}{dp} = \frac{1}{C''(x)}.$$

If $0 < C''(x) < \infty$, then $dx/dp > 0$. A shift from the Wald to the maximax criterion involves a change from

$$\text{Max}_x [p_1 x - C(x)] \text{ to } \text{Max}_x [p_n x - C(x)].$$

This change results in an increase of production which is

equivalent to that of a price increase of $\Delta p = p_n - p_1$ in the maximization case. Such a price change leads to a variation in production of $\Delta x = g(p_n) - g(p_1)$. By the theorem of the mean, $\Delta x = g(p_n) - g(p_1) = \int_{p_1}^{p_n} g'(p)\, dp = g'(\xi)\Delta p$, where ξ $= p_1 + \theta(p_n - p_1)$ and $0 < \theta < 1$. If $g'(p)$ is positive everywhere in the interval $p_1 \leq p \leq p_n$, it will be positive for $p = \xi$. Since our assumption is that $C''(x) > 0$ everywhere within the required interval, $g'(\xi) > 0$. Hence, if $\Delta p > 0$, $\Delta x > 0$. Therefore, a change from the Wald to the maximax criterion leads to an increase of output if the decision set consists of more than one price value. Similarly, in the above case, the Bayes optimal level of output can be shown to lie between the Wald and maximax levels.

From the above analysis and under the static decision assumptions, the supply functions for the one-product firm with certain costs are as follows:

Under certainty, the supply function is, if A.V.C. stands for average variable cost,

$$\begin{cases} x = S = g(p) & \text{for } p \geq \min \text{ A.V.C.} \\ x = S = 0 & \text{for } p < \min \text{ A.V.C.} \end{cases}$$

For the Wald criterion, it is

$$\begin{cases} x = S = g(p_1) & \text{for } p_1 \geq \min \text{ A.V.C.} \\ x = S = 0 & \text{for } p_1 < \min \text{ A.V.C.} \end{cases}$$

For the Bayes criterion, it is

$$\begin{cases} x = S = g(E[p]) & \text{for } E(p) \geq \min \text{ A.V.C.} \\ x = S = 0 & \text{for } E(p) < \min \text{ A.V.C.} \end{cases}$$

Finally, for the maximax criterion it is

$$\begin{cases} x = S = g(p_n) & \text{for } p_n \geq \min \text{ A.V.C.} \\ x = S = 0 & \text{for } p_n < \min \text{ A.V.C.} \end{cases}$$

In this static decision case, all of the supply functions are of identical *form*—supplies differ only insofar as they depend (or can be made to depend) upon different price values.

F. Comparisons of Production Under
Certainty and Uncertainty

Although levels of output for different criteria under uncertainty have been compared, these levels have not been compared with output under certainty. Let us make a few tentative comments upon such comparisons. Consider the above one-product model and suppose that in an interval of time the prices p_j, $j = 1, \ldots, n$, occur with the respective relative frequencies ρ_j, $j = 1, \ldots, n$. Then, the firm's average output under certainty is

$$\sum_{j=1}^{n} \rho_j g(p_j)$$

if it maximizes profit. We suppose that each of these prices exceeds minimum average variable cost, and that marginal cost is not perfectly inelastic.

Under uncertainty we suppose that the prices p_j occur with the (*known*) random probabilities ρ_j and that the probability distribution does not change in time. Random price values are treated as being independent. Under these assumptions the average Wald optimal level of output for uncertainty is less than under certainty since

$$g(p_1) < \sum_{j=1}^{n} \rho_j g(p_j)$$

because

$$g'(p) = \frac{1}{C''(x)} > 0.$$

Similarly, the average maximax level of output is higher than the average level under certainty. The situation is more complicated for Bayes' criterion. The average Bayesian level of optimal output under uncertainty is

$$g(E[p]) = g(\sum_{j=1}^{n} p_j p_j).$$

Now,

$$g(\sum_{j=1}^{n} p_j p_j) \gtreqless \sum_{j=1}^{n} p_j g(p_j)$$

accordingly as[6]

$$g''(p) \lesseqgtr 0.$$

Applying the inverse differentiation rule,

$$g''(p) \lesseqgtr 0,$$

accordingly as

$$C'''(x) \lesseqgtr 0.$$

If marginal cost increases at an increasing rate and the above conditions apply, then, for the Bayes criterion, average output will be less under uncertainty than under certainty.

E. Conclusion

The above relationship between the decision set of prices under uncertainty and actual prices is an extremely special one.[7] Nevertheless, similar relationships have been assumed in economic analysis of this sort. However, the assumption appears so narrow that its use in the absence of positive empirical evidence suggesting applicability should be restricted. In practice, the average minimax price value need not be equal to p_1 and could bear a wide range of relationships to actual price. Similarly, it may be possible to discover a wide range of relationships for the price values of other criteria. Therefore, the use of this particular assumption will be kept to a minimum and in the later part of the forthcoming analysis will not be used at all.

[6] G. H. Hardy, J. E. Littlewood, G. Polya: *Inequalities*, Cambridge University Press, Cambridge, 1934, pp. 74–75.

[7] In the above case the decision set coincides with the objectively possible prices on a relative frequency basis.

On the whole, considerations of changes of production optima have been restricted to the minimax, maximax, and Bayes criteria. It can be said that these criteria signify respectively a security, gambling, and average income bias on the part of the firm. However, I do not wish to suggest that these three criteria are the ones which are most frequently used under uncertainty. The frequency of the use of different criteria is an empirical question which is not to be settled without observation. Indeed, one of my hypotheses is that behavior is diverse under uncertainty and that it is unlikely that it can be represented by a few criteria. However, even if it is diverse, it can often be reduced to some common index problem.

In the above analysis, it is the conversion of diverse behavior results to equivalent maximization results which make the effects of diverse behavior readily comparable. This comparability is possible for diverse criteria and for diverse price forecasts, and it will enable us to comprehend a number of general theorems. In considering the conversion of apparent non-extremum problems into extremum ones, Samuelson concludes that "it is well to emphasize that the conversion of a problem whose economic context does not suggest only human, purposive, maximizing behavior into a maximum problem is to be regarded as merely a technical device for the purpose of quickly developing the properties of that equilibrium position."[8] Although the conversion is technical, at the same time it is not to be disparaged. The conversion establishes a general ordering device for different types of behavior under the static decision-making assumption.

Until there is strong empirical evidence to suggest that firms adopt only a limited number of criteria, it seems to be the correct course for *a priori* theories to embrace as wide a set of possibilities as may feasibly exist. Similarly, until further empirical evidence is forthcoming, a wide range of possible relations between decision prices and actual prices should be assumed.

[8] P. A. Samuelson, *op. cit.*, pp. 52-53.

CHAPTER V

Some Influences of Price
Uncertainty and Price
Instability Upon
the Firm's Average Profit

A. Introduction

It is sometimes suggested that increased price instability increases the firm's expected profit.[1] But such an increase only comes about under particular conditions, and it is one of the purposes of this chapter to indicate some of them. The pattern of price uncertainty or errors is not necessarily independent of price variability, and consequently, under certain conditions, increased price instability decreases expected profit.

However, this chapter deals with broader issues than this. It investigates, in a comparatively general way, the separate and combined effects of price uncertainty and price instability upon the one-product firm's average level of profit. A static decision-making assumption is employed, and the maximum equivalence proposition is used to increase generality.

A conflict arises in the development of the analysis. Generality in one direction needs to be sacrificed for simplicity in another. Increasing the generality of the cost functions increases the complexity of dealing with the influence of price uncertainty and instability. Given this problem, my choice has been to concentrate on a quadratic cost model in the body of the chapter and to state a few relationships which apply to more general functions in an appendix to the chapter.

---

[1] For instance, W. Oi claims that expected profit is greater the greater the degree of price instability. W. Y. Oi, "The Desirability of Price Instability under Perfect Competition," *Econometrica*, vol. 29 (1961), pp. 58–64, and W. Oi, "Rejoinder," *Econometrica*, vol. 31 (1963), p. 248.

Within the chapter, two models are considered. The first relies upon a general cost function but utilizes special assumptions about the distribution of actual prices and shadow prices; the second relies upon a quadratic total cost function but involves general assumptions about the distribution of actual prices and shadow prices. The first model, which is discussed in section B, is merely an illustrative example and, therefore, some readers may wish to omit it and turn to section C.

B. A Simple Model

The main purpose of this model is to illustrate the point that if price prediction errors arise increased price instability need not increase the firm's average profit. In this model, adjustments from planned output are ruled out for physical or cost reasons. The following assumptions are made:

(i) The firm wishes to maximize expected profit.

(ii) The marginal cost curve increases over the relevant range, and cost is certain.

(iii) The prices $(1 + a)p$ and $(1 - a)p$ each occur with a relative frequency of 0.5 under price certainty.

(iv) Under uncertainty the possible prices have a probability distribution which is the same as the relative frequency distribution of price under certainty. Under uncertainty, the producer knows that $(1 + a)p$ and $(1 - a)p$ each occur randomly, and that each has a probability of 0.5.

(v) Output is planned in period $t - n$, $n > 0$, for period t and is unalterable for physical or cost reasons.

We assume that expected price is stationary, that the cost function is the same through time, and that the decisions of each period are independent of those made in others. Decisions are independent but are unalterable once made in $t - n$. Given the above assumptions, a comparison can be made between the expected profit for a stable price of p and that for a situation of price instability where $(1 + a)p$ and $(1 - a)p$ are two prices, each of which occurs with a probability 0.5.

From this comparison, propositions can be shown to hold which conflict with the hypothesis that increased price instability increases expected profit. If π represents profit, if $C(x)$ represents total cost, and if a and b are parameters such that $0 < a < 1$ and $0 < b < 1$, the profit functions when price is $(1 - a)p$, p, and $(1 + a)p$ are:

$$\pi_1 = (1 - a)px - C(x) = f(x). \tag{5.1}$$

$$\pi_2 = px - C(x) = v(x). \tag{5.2}$$

$$\pi_3 = (1 + a)px - C(x) = h(x). \tag{5.3}$$

We assume the function $f(x)$ to reach a maximum at x_1, $v(x)$ to reach a maximum at x_2, and $h(x)$ to reach a maximum at x_3. Given that $0 < C'(x) < \infty$ for $x_1 \leq x \leq x_3$, then $x_1 < x_2 < x_3$ and $\pi_1 < \pi_2 < \pi_3$. Using these relations and two others to be specified later, it is possible to prove a number of propositions about expected profit.

Proposition (i): If price is uncertain and unstable, action which is intended to maximize profit at each instant may lead to a lower level of expected profit than when price is stable at p.

This will be so if the firm makes mistakes of a sufficient frequency and magnitude in its price forecasts. Suppose that with a probability of 0.25 the firm mistakenly predicts $(1 + a)p$ and that with the same probability it mistakenly predicts $(1 - a)p$. Then, if it acts on these predictions, its expected profit

$$0.25[f(x_1) + f(x_3) + h(x_1) + h(x_3)]$$

will be less than that for the stable price p, i.e.,

$$0.25[f(x_1) + f(x_3) + h(x_1) + h(x_3)] < v(x_2). \tag{5.4}$$

Proof: from equations 5.1, 5.2, and 5.3,

$$
\begin{aligned}
\text{L.H.S. of 5.4} &= 0.25\,[(1 - a)px_1 - C(x_1) + (1 - a)px_3 \\
&\quad - C(x_3) + (1 + a)px_1 - C(x_1) + (1 + a)px_3 \\
&\quad - C(x_3)] \\
&= 0.5[px_1 - C(x_1) + px_3 - C(x_3)] \\
&= 0.5[v(x_1) + v(x_3)]. \tag{5.5}
\end{aligned}
$$

But $v(x)$ reaches a unique maximum at x_2. Hence,

$$0.5[v(x_1) + v(x_3)] < v(x_2). \qquad 5.6$$

Q.E.D.

If the firm is just as likely to be right as wrong in forecasting the actual price in t, and if it adjusts to its forecasts in the hope of maximizing profit, an increase in the range of possible price will decrease expected profit. The firm's expected profit will be at a maximum when price is stable at p.

Proposition (ii): As the range of price variation increases, expected profit declines if the firm attempts to maximize at each instant and if its distribution of prediction errors is of the same form as the previous one.[2]

Although this proposition can be deduced from the previous argument, it can be easily supported by supposing that the prices $(1 - a - b)p$ and $(1 + a + b)p$ each occur with a probability of 0.5. The relevant profit functions are

$$\pi_0 = (1 - a - b)px - C(x) = e(x) \qquad 5.7$$

and

$$\pi_4 = (1 + a + b)px - C(x) = m(x) \qquad 5.8$$

Let these functions reach a maximum at x_0 and at x_4, respectively. If the firm mistakenly acts upon $(1 - a - b)p$ with a probability of 0.25 and mistakenly acts upon $(1 + a + b)p$ with the same probability, its expected profit,

$$0.25[e(x_0) + e(x_4) + m(x_0) + m(x_4)]$$

is less than in the two previous circumstances, i.e.,

$$0.25[e(x_0) + e(x_4) + m(x_0) + m(x_4)]$$
$$< 0.25[f(x_1) + f(x_3) + h(x_1) + h(x_3)] < v(x_2). \qquad 5.9$$

---

[2] It is not denied that increased price instability can increase expected profit if price is certain. This is shown generally in the appendix to this chapter. Also, given some error patterns, increased price instability increases expected profit.

Proof:

$$0.25[e(x_0) + e(x_4) + m(x_0) + m(x_4)] = 0.5[px_0 - C(x_0)$$
$$+ px_4 - C(x_4)] = 0.5[v(x_0) + v(x_4)]. \qquad 5.10$$

Now, $v(x)$ reaches a maximum at x_2, and $v'(x) > 0$ for $0 < x < x_2$, and $v'(x) < 0$ for $x > x_2$. Therefore, $v(x_0) < v(x_1) < v(x_2)$, and $v(x_4) < v(x_3) < v(x_2)$.

Hence,

$$0.5[v(x_0) + v(x_4)] < 0.5[v(x_1) + v(x_3)] < v(x_2). \qquad 5.11$$

Reference to equation 5.6 confirms that expression 5.11 is equivalent to expression 5.9, and the above proposition is confirmed.

Q.E.D.

Proposition (iii): If the firm constantly produces the output x_2 which maximizes profit for the average price p, then its expected profit will be greater than if it adjusts to its price forecasts.

This is supposing that expected price is stationary and that the firm's forecast errors have a distribution similar to the one mentioned previously. Expected profit from producing x_2 is $0.5[f(x_2) + h(x_2)]$, and the proposition asserts that

$$0.5[f(x_2) + h(x_2)] > 0.25[f(x_1)$$
$$+ f(x_3) + h(x_1) + h(x_3)]. \qquad 5.12$$

Proof:

$$0.5[f(x_2) + h(x_2)]$$
$$= 0.5[(1 - a)px_2 - C(x_2) + (1 + a)px_2 - C(x_2)]$$
$$= px_2 - C(x_2) = v(x_2).$$

From expression 5.9,

$$v(x_2) > 0.25[f(x_1) + f(x_3) + h(x_1) + h(x_3)].$$

Q.E.D.

It follows as a corollary to expression 5.12 that there are a number of output levels in the neighborhood of x_2 which, although second best, yield an expected profit in excess of that which is earned by adjusting to forecasts with the above probability distribution of errors. Briefly, this is so because $0.5[f(x_2) + h(x_2)] = v(x_2)$ and this value exceeds $0.25[f(x_1) + f(x_3) + h(x_1) + h(x_2)]$ by some positive amount and $v(x)$ is continuous.

Proposition (iv): If the firm constantly produces the output x_2 which maximizes profit for the average price p, its expected profit will be at a maximum.

Where x_α is any level of output, the expected profit associated with it is $0.5[f(x_\alpha) + h(x_\alpha)]$, and the above proposition asserts that

$$0.5[f(x_2) + h(x_2)] \geq 0.5[f(x_\alpha) + h(x_\alpha)]. \qquad 5.13$$

Proof:

$$0.5[f(x_\alpha) + h(x_\alpha)]$$
$$= 0.5[(1 - a)px_\alpha - C(x_\alpha) + (1 + a)px_\alpha - C(x_\alpha)]$$
$$= px_\alpha - C(x_\alpha) = v(x_\alpha). \qquad 5.14$$

Since $v(x)$ reaches a maximum at x_2, $v(x_\alpha)$ reaches a maximum at $x_\alpha = x_2$.

Q.E.D.

If expected price is stationary in time, expected profit will be maximized by holding output constant at the level which maximizes profit for the average price. Even if the probability of forecast error is lower than 0.25 for each price, it can still be more profitable for the firm to hold its production constant at an intermediate level rather than to adjust its output marginally in accordance with its price forecasts. This follows from expression 4.4, i.e.,

$$0.25[f(x_1) + f(x_3) + h(x_1) + h(x_3)] < v(x_2).$$

Proposition (v): The expected profit to be earned by constantly producing any level of output x_α is equal to the profit when price is stable at p because

$$0.5[f(x_\alpha) + h(x_\alpha)] = v(x_\alpha).$$

Proposition (vi): If production is held constant and if the mean price is stationary, expected profit does not decline as the range of price variation increases.

In fact, expected profit remains constant. This proposition contrasts with the forecast adjustment case, i.e., proposition (i). Proposition (vi) asserts that

$$0.5[f(x_\alpha) + h(x_\alpha)] = 0.5[e(x_\alpha) + m(x_\alpha)]. \qquad 5.15$$

Proof:

$$0.5[f(x_\alpha) + h(x_\alpha)]$$
$$= 0.5[(1 - a)px_\alpha - C(x_\alpha) + (1 + a)px_\alpha$$
$$-C(x_\alpha)] = px_\alpha - C(x_\alpha). \qquad 5.16$$

$$0.5[e(x_\alpha) + m(x_\alpha)]$$
$$= 0.5[(1 - a - b)px_\alpha - C(x_\alpha) + (1 + a + b)px_\alpha$$
$$-C(x_\alpha)] = px_\alpha - C(x_\alpha). \qquad 5.17$$

$$\text{Q.E.D.}$$

Propositions (iv) to (vi) inclusive can be generalized for any probability distribution of price with a stationary value of expected price. Let $E(p)$ be the expected price of such a probability distribution. Then, under uncertainty, expected profit is

$$E(\pi) = E[px - C(x)]$$
$$= E[p]x - C(x) \qquad 5.18$$

because the output of $t - n$ is unalterable. Let the maximum of this function occur for $x = \hat{x}$. Now, if price is stable at $\bar{p} = E[p]$, profit will be

$$\pi = \bar{p}x - C(x). \qquad 5.19$$

But since $\bar{p} = E[p]$, expression 5.19 equals expression 5.18. Hence,

$$\text{Max}_{x} E(\pi) = \bar{p}\hat{x} - C(\hat{x})$$
$$= \text{Max}_{x} [\bar{p}x - C(x)]. \qquad 5.20$$

In this particular model certainty equivalence exists, and, if expected price is constant, changes in the probability distribution of price do not affect the level of maximum expected profit and the level of optimal output. If expected price remains constant and if production is held constant at any level, increased price instability will leave expected profit unchanged. The expected profit from any level of output x_α is

$$E(\pi) = E(p)x_\alpha - C(x_\alpha). \qquad 5.21$$

If both $E(p)$ and x_α are constant while the price variance increases, $E(\pi)$ is constant.

From the above model, it is clear that the hypothesis that increased price instability leads to an increase in expected profit requires qualification. Under the conditions of this model, increased price instability does not lead to a greater level of expected profit than is earnable with a stable price, and, to maximize expected profit, it is necessary to hold production constant if expected price is constant. There are also a number of constant outputs in the neighborhood of the optimum for maximizing expected profit which, although "second best," enable higher expected profit to be earned than by varying production in accordance with one's imperfect forecasts. The desirability of constancy arises from the constancy of expected price and the fact that expected profits will be decreased by attempting to forecast and adjust to random movements.

An assumption underlying the above analysis is that the firm at least knows the objective level of expected price.[3] In practice, the firm will be forced to act upon a subjective estimate of expected price which may or may not accord with the objective level. If the subjective estimate remains stationary and the firm acts upon it to maximize subjective expected profit, then its level of optimal output will remain stationary but its objective level of expected profit will increase, decrease, or remain stationary accordingly as the objective level of expected price increases, decreases, or remains stationary. It is

[3] This assumption is relaxed to obtain proposition (ii).

obvious then that the underlying assumption of non-divergence between the subjective and objective level of expected price can limit the practical application of the above expected profit theorems. In the concluding model of this chapter (see section D) we shall drop this assumption.

C. A Measure of Price Uncertainty

Before dealing with the next production model, let us discuss some possible measures of price uncertainty. There seems to be no agreed unique measure of this phenomenon, but let us consider the following measures as possibilities. In these measures, E represents expected or average values, p represents the actual price of the product and $\hat{p}$ its shadow price, R denotes the correlation coefficient of p and $\hat{p}$, and σ and cov represent the standard deviation and covariance respectively.

(i) $$-\text{cov}(p, \hat{p}) = -E\{[p - E(p)][\hat{p} - E(\hat{p})]\}. \qquad 5.22$$

(ii) $$-R = -\frac{\text{cov}(p, \hat{p})}{\sigma_p \sigma_{\hat{p}}}. \qquad 5.23$$

(iii) $$1 - R^2. \qquad 5.24$$

(iv) $$E\{(p - \hat{p})^2\}. \qquad 5.25$$

Consider these measures in turn. The negative of the covariance of price and shadow price $-\text{cov}(p, \hat{p})$ is variable for proportional changes of the price values. If the p values increase by the fraction λ and the $\hat{p}$ values increase by the fraction θ, $-\text{cov}(p, \hat{p})$ changes to $-\lambda\theta\text{cov}(p, \hat{p})$. Also, the value of $-\text{cov}(p, \hat{p})$ can be arbitrarily influenced by the units of measurement. But this problem can be overcome by expressing $\text{cov}(p, \hat{p})$ in deviation units so that the measure of uncertainty becomes

$$-R = -\frac{\text{cov}(p, \hat{p})}{\sigma_p \sigma_{\hat{p}}}.$$

The measure $1 - R^2$ does not vary with proportional price changes, but it is unsatisfactory as a general measure of price uncertainty because it implies that price uncertainty is the same for positive and negative R-values of equal absolute magnitude.

It implies that uncertainty is zero if $R = -1$, but differences between shadow and actual prices certainly occur in this case.

The measure $E(p - \hat{p})^2$ is the mean of the square of the deviations of shadow price from actual price. More fully,

$$M = E[(p - \hat{p})^2]$$

$$= [E(p) - E(\hat{p})]^2 + \sigma_p^2 - 2 \operatorname{cov}(p, \hat{p}) + \sigma_{\hat{p}}^2 \quad 5.26$$

$$= [E(p) - E(\hat{p})]^2 + \sigma_{p-\hat{p}}^2 \quad 5.27$$

where $\sigma_{p-\hat{p}}^2$ is the variance of $p - \hat{p}$. This measure is not independent of proportional changes of price or of changes in the units of measurement. The mean square of relative deviations of actual price from shadow price,

$$E\left\{\left[\frac{p - \hat{p}}{p}\right]^2\right\} = E\left\{1 - \frac{2\hat{p}}{p} + \frac{\hat{p}^2}{p^2}\right\}$$

$$= 1 - E[2\hat{p}]E\left[\frac{1}{p}\right] - 2 \operatorname{cov}\left(\hat{p}, \frac{1}{p}\right) + E\left[\frac{\hat{p}}{p}\right]^2 + \operatorname{var}\left[\frac{\hat{p}}{p}\right],$$

$$5.28$$

is, in this respect, a more satisfactory measure, but unlike M, it is algebraically difficult to apply it to profit analysis.[4] M will be used to measure price uncertainty in the next model.

D. An Average Profit Model which is Based on a Quadratic Cost Function but allows for more Generality in the Distribution of Actual and Shadow Price Values

In order to consider more systematically the separate and combined effects of price uncertainty and instability upon

---

[4] In some formulations uncertainty is measured by the entropy formula. If p_j is the probability of the price p_j, $j = 1, \ldots, n$, and if $\Sigma_j p_j = 1$, then the entropy value is

$$H(p_1, p_2, \ldots, p_n) = - \sum_{j=1}^{n} p_j \log p_j.$$

Increases in $H(p_1, p_2, \ldots, p_n)$ indicate increases in uncertainty. Some implications of the formula are outlined by A. I. Khinchin, *Mathematical* average profit, let us make the following assumptions:

(i) The firm's output in t equals the output which it "plans" for t in $t - n$, $n \geq 1$.

(ii) The output of any period is independent of that of any other.

(iii) Costs are certain and stationary.

(iv) Total cost is a quadratic function of output x. Where C represents total cost, and $a > 0$, $b \gtrless 0$, $C = ax^2 + bx + c$.

Given these assumptions, the firm's profit function for any period can be expressed as

$$\pi = px - (ax^2 + bx + c), \qquad 5.29$$

where p is the actual price realized in the period. This profit function can also be expressed in terms of actual and "shadow" prices. If $\hat{p}$ denotes the "shadow" price of the product, than a unique $\hat{p}$-value exists such that

$$x = \frac{\hat{p} - b}{2a}. \qquad 5.30$$

where $\hat{p}$ is the solution of 5.30, the profit function can be expressed as

$$\pi = p\left(\frac{\hat{p} - b}{2a}\right) - \left[a\left(\frac{\hat{p} - b}{2a}\right)^2 + b\left(\frac{\hat{p} - b}{2a}\right) + c\right]. \qquad 5.31$$

Consequently, average profit,[5] i.e., profit averaged over several

---

Foundations of Information Theory, Dover Publications, New York, 1959. The formula has been applied to economic decision making by J. Marschak in "Remarks on the Economics of Information," *Cowles Foundation Discussion Paper*, No. 70, 1959.

[5] Since the following equation is based on shadow prices, it is apparent from our discussion in Chapters IV and V that this equation is very general. The $\hat{p}$ values might correspond to expected prices, minimax prices, etc.

periods, is

$$E(\pi)$$

$$= \frac{E(p)E(\hat{p}) + \text{cov}(p, \hat{p}) - bE(p)}{2a} - c$$

$$- b\frac{E(\hat{p}) - b}{2a} - \frac{E(\hat{p})^2 + \text{var}\,\hat{p} - 2bE(\hat{p}) + b^2}{4a}$$

$$= \frac{2E(p)E(\hat{p}) + 2\,\text{cov}(p, \hat{p}) - 2bE(p) - E(\hat{p})^2 - \text{var}\,\hat{p} + b^2}{4a} - c.$$

$$5.32$$

A number of general propositions about the influence of price uncertainty and instability can be derived by using equation 5.32 if we let M measure the degree of price uncertainty and the variance of price σ_p^2, measure price instability. First, let us consider a few relationships without putting any particular restrictions upon the interdependence of the moments in 5.32.

If the average value of actual price $E(p)$ is constant, then, from equation 5.32,

$$\Delta E(\pi)$$

$$= \frac{1}{4a}\{[2E(p) - 2E(\hat{p})]\Delta E(\hat{p}) + 2\Delta\text{cov}(p, \hat{p}) - \Delta\text{var}\hat{p}\}$$

$$= -\frac{1}{4a}\{[-2E(p) + 2E(\hat{p})]\Delta E(\hat{p}) - 2\Delta\,\text{cov}(p, \hat{p}) + \Delta\sigma_{\hat{p}}^2\}.$$

$$5.33$$

Also, if $E(p)$ is constant, it follows from equation 5.26 that

$$\Delta M = [-2E(p) + 2E(\hat{p})]\Delta E(\hat{p}) + \Delta\sigma_p^2$$

$$- 2\Delta\,\text{cov}(p, \hat{p}) + \Delta\sigma_{\hat{p}}^2. \quad 5.34$$

Consequently, if $E(p)$ and σ_p^2 are constant, equation 5.33 becomes

$$\Delta E(\pi) = -\frac{1}{4a}\Delta M, \quad 5.35$$

and, given these conditions,

$$\Delta E(\pi) \lesseqgtr 0$$

as

$$\Delta M \gtreqless 0.$$

If the average value of price and the variance of price is constant, average profit increases with decreased price uncertainty as measured by M, the mean square of the deviations of shadow price from actual. Given these conditions, average profit varies inversely with price uncertainty; it changes by the negative value of the reciprocal of twice the rate of change of marginal cost times the change of M.

Now, let us consider the effect upon average profit of an increase in price instability, the "degree" of price uncertainty M, and the average value of actual price assumed to be constant. Specifically, let us consider the effect upon $E(\pi)$ of an increase in the variance of price, σ_p^2, if $E(p)$ and M remain constant. Since by our assumptions, $\Delta M = 0$ and $E(p)$ is constant,

$$\Delta M = [-2E(p) + 2E(\hat{p})]\Delta E(\hat{p}) + \Delta \sigma_p^2 - 2\Delta \, \text{cov}\,(p,\hat{p}) \\ + \Delta \sigma_{\hat{p}}^2 = 0. \qquad 5.36$$

Rearranging,

$$[-2E(p) + 2E(\hat{p})]\Delta E(\hat{p}) - 2\Delta \, \text{cov}\,(p,\hat{p}) + \Delta \sigma_{\hat{p}}^2 = -\Delta \sigma_p^2. \\ 5.37$$

Hence, substituting in equation 5.33,

$$\Delta E(\pi) = \frac{1}{4a} \Delta \sigma_p^2. \qquad 5.38$$

Consequently, if $E(p)$ and M are constant,

$$\Delta E(\pi) \gtreqless 0$$

as

$$\Delta \sigma_p^2 \gtreqless 0.$$

If the average value of price and the "degree" of price uncertainty M are constant, average profit increases with increased price instability as measured by the variance of price. In fact, under these conditions, an increase in the price variance increases average profit by the reciprocal of twice the rate of change of marginal cost times the increase in the variance of price.

In order to integrate some existing theories into this framework, it is necessary to consider the restrictions which these theories place upon the interrelationship of the moments in equation 5.32. By relating the moments in particular ways, we shall obtain some additional insights into the effects of price instability upon average profit.

E. Restrictions upon the Relationship between the Moments of the Average Profit Function

Assume that for the "population" of $\hat{p}$-values, the least squares regression of p on $\hat{p}$ is given by

$$z = \gamma_0 + \gamma_1 \hat{p}. \qquad 5.39$$

Then, this relationship restricts the moments of equation 5.32. From the theory of regression analysis,[6] the "explained"

variance of p is

$$\sigma_z^2 = \gamma_1^2 \sigma_{\hat{p}}^2. \qquad 5.40$$

Also,

$$\sigma_z^2 = R^2 \sigma_p^2. \qquad 5.41$$

Therefore, using these two equations,

$$\sigma_{\hat{p}}^2 = \frac{R^2 \sigma_p^2}{\gamma_1^2} = \frac{\sigma_z^2}{\gamma_1^2}. \qquad 5.42$$

[6] See, for example, C. E. Weatherburn, *A First Course in Mathematical Statistics*, The University Press, Cambridge, 1961. Especially Ch. IV.

This result can also be used to express the covariance of price and shadow price in terms of its restrictions.

$$\begin{aligned}
\operatorname{cov}(p, \hat{p}) &= R\sigma_p\sigma_{\hat{p}} \\
&= R\sigma_p \left(\frac{R^2}{\gamma_1^2}\sigma_p^2\right)^{\frac{1}{2}} \\
&= \frac{R^2\sigma_p^2}{\gamma_1} = \frac{\sigma_z^2}{\gamma_1}.
\end{aligned}$$

5.43

Now, we may substitute for $\sigma_{\hat{p}}^2$ and $\operatorname{cov}(p, \hat{p})$ in equation 5.32, using equations 5.42 and 5.43. We obtain the restricted relationship,

$E(\pi)$

$$= \frac{2E(p)E(\hat{p}) + \dfrac{2R^2}{\gamma_1}\sigma_p^2 - 2bE(p) - E(\hat{p})^2 - \dfrac{R^2}{\gamma_1^2}\sigma_p^2 + b}{4a} - c.$$

5.44

This equation clears up some confusion.

Oi has mentioned the possibility of relating actual and predicted prices (in our case shadow prices) by means of regression analysis and has concluded: "If the explained variance [of actual price] is positive, then it can be shown that greater systematic fluctuations in prices must increase expected profits. Space precludes a full proof of this proposition ... so long as price instability contains a systematic component, greater price instability will lead to higher expected profits."[7] Since Oi states that the explained variance of price represents the systematic component, his conclusion restated is: so long as the explained variance of price is positive, greater price instability will lead to higher expected profit.

However, a positive explained variance is not sufficient for this result. This is, at once, clear if we suppose that $E(p)$, $E(\hat{p})$, and σ_z^2 do not change with actual price but σ_z^2 is positive. Working from expressions 5.42 and 5.43 and substituting into 5.32, we see that expected profit remains constant in this case.

---

[7] W. Oi, "Rejoinder," p. 248.

Even if the correlation coefficient R is positive and constant, with the above regression line maintained, increased price instability does not necessarily increase average profit.

Let us show this. *Assume* that $\Delta R = 0$, $\Delta E(p) = 0$, $\Delta E(\hat{p}) = 0$; i.e., the correlation coefficient, average level of prices, and the average level of shadow prices remain constant. Then, from equation 5.44,

$$\Delta E(\pi) = \left[\frac{R^2}{2a\gamma_1} - \frac{R^2}{4a\gamma_1^2} \right] \Delta\sigma_p^2 \qquad 5.45$$

$$= \left[\frac{R^2(2\gamma_1 - 1)}{4a\gamma_1^2} \right] \Delta\sigma_p^2 \qquad 5.46$$

Hence, if $R \neq 0$,

$$\frac{\partial E(\pi)}{\partial\sigma_p^2} \gtreqless 0$$

as

$$\gamma_1 = \frac{\text{cov}\,(p, \hat{p})}{\sigma_{\hat{p}}^2} \gtreqless \frac{1}{2}.$$

This enables us to show that, even if $R > 0$, average profit can decrease with increases in the variance of price. Since, from equation 5.42,

$$\gamma_1 = \frac{R\sigma_p}{\sigma_{\hat{p}}}, \qquad 5.47$$

equation 5.45 can be written as

$$\Delta E(\pi) = \left[\frac{R^2 \left(\dfrac{2R\sigma_p}{\sigma_{\hat{p}}} - 1 \right)}{4a\gamma_1^2} \right] \Delta\sigma_p^2. \qquad 5.48$$

Consequently,

$$\frac{\partial E(\pi)}{\partial\sigma_p^2} \gtreqless 0$$

as

$$\sigma_{\hat{p}} \gtreqless 2R\sigma_p,$$

and, therefore, since $0.5\sigma_{\hat{p}}$ may exceed $R\sigma_p$, average profit can decrease with increases in the price variance. For this result, we suppose R, $E(p)$, and $E(\hat{p})$ to be constant. *Hence, a systematic component in the form of a positive and constant correlation coefficient does not ensure that increased price instability increases average profit.*

Specifically, in the above case, if the standard deviation of the shadow price exceeds the standard deviation of actual price times twice the correlation coefficient, average profit declines if there is an increase in the standard deviation of price. Or, again if the slope of the regression line, i.e., γ_1, is less than 0.5 and remains constant, an increase in the variance of price decreases average profit, R, $E(p)$, and $E(\hat{p})$ remaining unchanged. So, although increased price instability raises average profit under a variety of conditions, a positive and constant correlation coefficient of actual and shadow prices does not ensure such an increase.

Assuming a constant regression line as set out in expression 5.39, let us consider the effect upon average profit of a variation in R^2 supposing the average value of actual prices, the average value of shadow prices, and the variance of actual price to be constant. If $\Delta E(p) = 0$, if $E(\hat{p}) = 0$, and if $\Delta\sigma_p^2 = 0$, it follows from equation 5.44 that

$$\Delta E(\pi) = \left[\frac{\left(\dfrac{2}{\gamma_1} - \dfrac{1}{\gamma_1^2}\right)\sigma_p^2}{4a}\right] \Delta R^2. \qquad 5.49$$

Consequently, given these conditions, if $\sigma_p^2 > 0$ and $2a < \infty$,

$$\frac{\partial E(\pi)}{\partial R^2} \gtreqless 0$$

as

$$\gamma_1 = \frac{\text{Cov}\,(p, \hat{p})}{\sigma_{\hat{p}}^2} \gtreqless 0.5.$$

If the average value of prices, the average value of shadow prices, and the variance of actual price are constant, an increase in coefficient of linear correlation does not necessarily raise expected profit.

However, it is of interest to note that under these conditions an increase of R^2 does not imply a decrease in the measure of price uncertainty M. Taking account of the linear regression restrictions imposed upon expression 5.26,

$$M = [E(p) - E(\hat{p})]^2 + \sigma_p{}^2 - \frac{2R^2\sigma_p{}^2}{\gamma_1} + \frac{R^2\sigma_p{}^2}{\gamma_1{}^2}. \qquad 5.50$$

Hence, if $\Delta E(p) = 0$, if $\Delta E(\hat{p}) = 0$, and if $\Delta \sigma_p{}^2 = 0$,

$$\Delta M = \left[\left(-\frac{2}{\gamma_1} + \frac{1}{\gamma_1{}^2}\right)\sigma_p{}^2\right]\Delta R^2. \qquad 5.51$$

This being so, if $\sigma_p{}^2 > 0$, $(\partial M/\partial R^2) \lesseqgtr 0$ as $\gamma_1 \gtreqless 0.5$. Consequently, our results accord with the general conclusions in section D.

A side point which follows from equation 5.49 is that if $\gamma_1 < 0.5$, the firm will increase its average profit by reducing R^2 to zero if $E(p)$, $E(\hat{p})$, and $\sigma_p{}^2$ are assumed to be constant. This reduction can be accomplished by making $\hat{p}$ always equal to the $E(\hat{p})$ value, i.e., by rigidly predicting the same price. It can also be done by suitably randomizing the $\hat{p}$ values so as to eliminate linear correlation and leave $E(\hat{p})$ unchanged. These propositions follow from the fact that if $R^2 = 0$, then $\text{cov}(p, \hat{p}) = E\{[E(p) - p][E(\hat{p}) - \hat{p}]\} = 0$. Hence, in these circumstances, two very different sorts of policies can effectively raise average profit. We see that even if $R > 0$ it can be more profitable for the firm not to attempt to predict variations of price and adjust for them but to rigidly predict the same price and produce the same quantity of output over a stretch of time.

F. Nelson's Model as a Special Case

Nelson's model[8] can be interpreted as a special case of the

[8] R. R. Nelson, "Uncertainty Prediction and Competitive Equilibrium," *The Quarterly Journal of Economics*, vol. 75 (1961) pp. 41–62. Also T. Marschak and R. Nelson, "Flexibility, Uncertainty and Economic Theory," *Metroeconomica*, vol. 14 (1962), pp. 42–58.

model of the last section. If we suppose, as Nelson has done, that $\hat{p}$ is an unbiased estimate of p, the regression of p on $\hat{p}$, i.e., equation 5.39, specializes to

$$z = \hat{p}. \qquad\qquad 5.52$$

Hence, since $\gamma_1 = 0$ and $E(p) = E(\hat{p})$ in Nelson's model, equation 5.44 can be reduced by substitution to give Nelson's basic equation,[9]

$$E(\pi) = \frac{R^2\sigma_p{}^2 + [E(p) - b]^2}{4a} - c. \qquad\qquad 5.53$$

Nelson derives a number of theorems from this equation. First, if $E(p)$ and R^2 are constant,

$$\Delta E(\pi) = \left(\frac{1}{4a} R^2\right) \Delta\sigma_p{}^2. \qquad\qquad 5.54$$

If $R^2 > 0$ and if $2a > \infty$, $\partial E(\pi)/\partial\sigma_p{}^2 > 0$. If the average value of price is constant and if R^2 is constant and positive, an increase in the variance of price increases average profit, and the less steep the slope of the marginal cost curve the greater is the rise for a given increase in the variance. In this model, an increase in the price variance increases average profit, but in the general linear regression case average profit may decline with an increase in the price variance.

Secondly, taking this model, consider the effect upon average profit of an increase in the linear correlation coefficient. If the average value of price $E(p)$ and the variance of price $\sigma_p{}^2$ are constant,

$$\Delta E(\pi) = \left(\frac{1}{4a} \sigma_p{}^2\right) \Delta R^2. \qquad\qquad 5.55$$

Consequently, if $2a < \infty$ and if $\sigma_p{}^2 > 0$, $\partial E(\pi)/\partial R^2 > 0$. In this case, average profit increases with increases in the value R^2. Therefore, it differs from the general linear case since in that case, as we observed, it is possible for average profit to

[9] Equation 5.53 corresponds to equation (3.7a) of Marschak and Nelson's article, *op. cit.*

decline with increases in R^2. However, in this special case, an increase of $1 - R^2$ always implies an increase in the measure of uncertainty M. This follows since, from equation 5.50, if $\gamma_1 = 0$, $\partial M/\partial R^2 = -\sigma_p{}^2$ and therefore $\partial M/[\partial(1 - R^2)] = \sigma_p{}^2 > 0$. We see that in this special case M varies inversely with R^2, but it does not necessarily do this in the general linear regression case.

G. Conclusion

It has been shown that increased price instability can decrease average profit even if there is a "systematic component" in the instability and that an increase in the correlation coefficient of actual and shadow prices may cause average profit to fall. Furthermore, in the quadratic cost case, it has been possible to present a general formulation and show successive specializations of it, finally arriving at some existing theories as special cases. Although the quadratic cost function allowed us to consider aspects of price uncertainty and price instability in simple quantitative terms, we should not lose sight of the fact that simply from the convexity of the cost functions we can deduce *some* theorems about the effects of price uncertainty and instability upon average profit. Some such theorems will be outlined in the appendix to this chapter.

APPENDIX TO CHAPTER V

Average Profit and a
General Cost Model

A conflict arises in dealing with the effect of price instability and uncertainty upon average profit. The more general the cost function, the more difficult it is to analyze the effect upon the firm's average profit of changes in the distribution of actual and shadow prices. However, under general cost conditions it is possible to derive the effect upon average profit of special changes in the distribution of actual and shadow prices. In order to obtain the effect of a special change, we shall use the relationship between maximum profit and price.

Let $\psi(p)$ represent profit as a function of price when output is adjusted to price so that a global maximum of profit exists. The function $\psi(p)$ is obtained in the following way:
If

$$\pi = px - C(x) \qquad \text{A5.1}$$

represents the firm's general profit function and if its production ceases when average variable cost is not covered, its supply function is

$$\left. \begin{array}{ll} x = g(p) & \text{for } p \geq \min \text{ A.V.C.} \\ x = 0 & \text{for } p < \min \text{ A.V.C.} \end{array} \right\} \qquad \text{A5.2}$$

Expression A5.2 is the inverse of[1]

$$\left. \begin{array}{ll} p = C'(x) & \text{for } p \geq \min \text{ A.V.C.} \\ 0 = x & \text{for } p < \min \text{ A.V.C.} \end{array} \right\} \qquad \text{A5.3}$$

---

[1] Average variable cost is assumed to reach a unique minimum at $x°$. For output values in excess of $x°$, the marginal cost function is assumed to increase monotonically.

When we substitute expression A5.2 into A5.1, maximum profit as a function of price is

$$\psi(p) = pg(p) - C(g[p]) \quad \text{for } p \geq \text{min A.V.C.}$$
$$\psi(p) = -K \qquad\qquad \text{for } p < \text{min A.V.C.}$$
$$\text{A5.4}$$

where K represents fixed cost. The rate of change of $\psi(p)$ for $p > \text{min A.V.C.}$ is

$$\frac{d\psi}{dp} = \frac{dg}{dp} + g(p) - \frac{dC}{dg}\frac{dg}{dp}$$

$$= \frac{dg}{dp}\left(p - \frac{dC}{dg}\right) + g(p) \qquad \text{A5.5}$$

$$= g(p)$$

because profit maximization requires that

$$p = \frac{dC}{dx} = \frac{dC}{dg(p)}.$$

By the inverse rule of differentiation, the slope of the maximum profit function is

$$\frac{d\psi}{dp} = g(p) = \frac{1}{C'(x)} \quad \text{for } p > \text{min A.V.C.}$$
$$\frac{d\psi}{dp} = 0 \qquad\qquad \text{for } p < \text{min A.V.C.}$$
$$\text{A5.6}$$

Consequently,

$$\frac{d^2\psi}{dp^2} = g'(p) = \frac{1}{C''(x)} \quad \text{for } p > \text{min A.V.C.}$$
$$\frac{d^2\psi}{dp^2} = 0 \qquad\qquad \text{for } p < \text{min A.V.C.}$$
$$\text{A5.7}$$

If we assume that $C''(x) > 0$ for all output values in excess of minimum average variable cost then $d^2\psi/dp^2 > 0$ for $p > \text{min A.V.C.}$ For price values in excess of minimum average variable cost, the maximum profit function increases at an increasing rate.

Because the function $\psi(p)$ is strictly convex for $p > $ min A.V.C., then, if $p > $ min A.V.C. and if all values of p are not equal,[2]

$$\psi\left(\sum_j \rho_j p_j\right) < \sum_j \rho_j \psi(p_j) \qquad \text{A5.8}$$

where ρ_j represents the probability (relative frequency) of the jth possible price of the product or, in slightly more general form,

$$\psi(E[p]) < E[\psi(p)]. \qquad \text{A5.9}$$

Expression A5.9 implies that *average profit is less for a known stable price of E[p] than for a known unstable price* having an average value of $E[p]$. This is so if $\psi(p)$ is strictly convex over the relevant range. This will be so if the marginal cost function for output values in excess of minimum average cost increases monotonically at an increasing rate, i.e., if it is strictly convex for these output values.

Expression A5.9 has another implication. Suppose that the distribution of price values remains unchanged and that the firm is reduced from the state where it knows the time of occurrence of each of the price values well in advance to the position where it only knows the expected value of these prices. No uncertainty exists in the first situation, but price uncertainty does exist in the second one. Expression A5.9 implies that *average profit is less* in the second situation, *the more uncertain* situation, since $\psi(p)$ is assumed to be strictly convex over the relevant range.

In the above discussion, it has been implicitly assumed that the production assumptions of section D of Chapter V hold, except that now the cost function is allowed to assume more general forms than a quadratic. We see that merely from a knowledge of convexity properties of cost functions, some indication of the effect of price uncertainty and price instability upon average profit is possible.

[2] See theorem 90, G. H. Hardy, J. E. Littlewood, and G. Polya, *Inequalities*, Cambridge University Press, 1934, p. 74.

CHAPTER VI

Flexibility, Average Profit, and Technique Choice

A. Introduction

Words in common usage often fail to distinguish between all phenomena or gradations of them, and this sometimes causes confusion in scientific work. Frequently, the progress of science requires that the meaning of existing words be refined and new terms invented. Already, in dealing with uncertain phenomena, we have encountered a number of semantic inadequacies in the term, "uncertainty." Similar inadequacies occur for the term "flexibility."

In everyday usage, if something is flexible this roughly means that it can be easily varied. But for economic analysis this meaning is inadequate, since ease of variation can be described by many different characteristics. It is of some importance to distinguish these characteristics for, as will be seen, they can have different consequences. For example, it is sometimes asserted that increased price uncertainty encourages the adoption of more flexible techniques. While there is little need to doubt this hypothesis if flexibility is defined so as to accord with Hart's[1] usage, this is not so if flexibility is defined so as to accord with the Baumol's[2] apparent usage.

For Hart,[3] flexiblity refers to the ability to modify plans in time. A plan is flexible if it is possible to diverge from the planned values at a date subsequent to their acceptance. If the firm plans a particular value of output (a point value),

[1] A. G. Hart, "Risk, Uncertainty and the Unprofitability of Compounding Probabilities," pp. 110–118 in *Studies in Mathematical Economics and Econometrics*, O. Lange, F. McIntyre and F. Yntema, eds., The University of Chicago Press, Chicago, 1942.
[2] W. J. Baumol, *Economic Dynamics*, 2nd edn., The Macmillan Company, New York, 1959, pp. 92 and 93.
[3] Hart, *op. cit.*

its plan is flexible if it can subsequently produce an output different from the planned. In Theil's terminology,[4] inflexible plans involve static decision-making, and flexible plans involve dynamic decision-making.

It seems that for both Stigler and Baumol flexibility refers to the rate of change of marginal cost when static decision-making is assumed. Under this condition, a technique is considered to be more inflexible the larger its second derivative of total cost.[5]

B. Baumol's Approach to Changes in Technique Choice

Baumol argues that "the existence of uncertainty will lead to the (increased) use of equipment whose scale of operation is flexible".[6] His argument is based upon a figure which is identical to Figure 6.1. In this figure, the average cost function of the inflexible technique is shown by AC_I and that of the flexible is shown by AC_F. Figure 6.1 is also identical with the one which G. J. Stigler uses in putting forward his hypothesis that under certainty increased price instability increases the likelihood of the firm's adopting the flexible technique.[7] In Figure 6.1 the second derivative of average cost of technique I exceeds that of technique F for all values of output.

Baumol's argument is along the following lines: Given the existence of complete price certainty, suppose the firm finds that an output between $0m$ and $0q$ is optimal. Then, it will minimize its costs by adopting technique I. If the firm becomes uncertain of its price, then it is possible for an output greater than $0q$ to be optimal, and in that event, technique F will minimize the firm's costs. Upon the basis of these observations, it is concluded that "the existence of uncertainty will lead to the

[4] H. Theil, *Economic Forecasts and Policy*, 2nd revised edn., North-Holland Publishing Company, Amsterdam, 1961, p. 372.

[5] Cf. T. Marschak and R. Nelson, "Flexibility, Uncertainty and Economic Theory," *Metroeconomica*, vol. 14 (1962), p. 49.

[6] Baumol, *op. cit.*

[7] G. J. Stigler, "Production and Distribution in the Short Run," *Journal of Political Economy*, vol. 47 (1939), pp. 305–328.

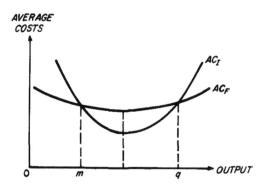

FIG. 6.1

use of equipment whose scale of operation is flexible." But this conclusion is reached by a very tenuous argument. However, it might be implicit in the argument that, under certainty and due to the operation of long-run entry, price will be in the neighborhood of minimum average cost and that this will not necessarily be so if uncertainty exists. Unfortunately, the argument is not very explicit and, as it stands, involves some speculation as to its contents. Indeed, as will be shown, if we indicate flexibility by the rate of change of marginal cost, then, under comparatively general conditions, increased price uncertainty increases the likelihood that the inflexible technique will be adopted.

For Baumol and Stigler, differences in the rate of change of marginal cost seem to distinguish flexible techniques from inflexible ones; the greater the rate change of a technique's marginal cost, the more inflexible it is. Maintaining this differentia, I shall introduce two models which indicate

    (i) that increased price uncertainty raises the likelihood of the firm's adopting an inflexible technique, and

(ii) that increased price instability, "price uncertainty constant," increases the likelihood of the firm's adopting a flexible technique.

The first model is an introductory one and is put forward because it relies upon a general cost relationship and not a quadratic one. The second model relies upon the assumption of a linear marginal cost function but enables us to treat the uncertainty aspect of the problem more generally.

C. Model I—A Simple Model

In Model I, we consider how the difference in the comparative profitability of two techniques changes as price changes from certain to probable. We attempt to isolate, under general cost conditions, a cost factor which has an important bearing upon the direction of technique choice as price changes from certain to probable. The following assumptions are made for Model I:

(i) Under uncertainty, the probability distribution of price is the same as the relative frequency distribution of price under certainty. The probability distribution is stationary in time.

(ii) The firm wishes to maximize expected profit.

(iii) Under uncertainty, the firm has perfect predictability of expected price.

(iv) The two techniques to be considered have the same length of life of N periods.

(v) Only one technique can be chosen for the N periods.

(vi) All the N periods are of equal length.

(vii) The marginal cost functions of every period are equal for each technique. This is also the case for the average cost functions.

(viii) After reaching their minimum, the marginal cost functions increase monotonically.

Also, the static decision-making assumptions of previous chapters are maintained:

    (ix) Output decisions for each period must be made prior to that period and, once made, are unalterable.

    (x) The output decisions which are made at different points of time are independent.

In order to develop the argument, let us derive the function which expresses the difference in the maximum profitability of the two techniques as a function of price. From the appendix of the previous chapter, various properties of maximum profit as a function of price are already known. For both techniques these functions are constant up to the level of minimum average variable cost and then increase at an increasing rate. Using the subscripts 1 and 2 to indicate techniques one and two, technique one's maximum profit function is[8]

$$\psi_1(p) = pg_1(p) - C(g_1[p]) \qquad \text{for } p \geq \text{min A.V.C.}_1$$
$$\psi_1(p) = -K_1 \qquad\qquad\quad \text{for } p < \text{min A.V.C.}_1$$

6.1

and

$$\psi_1'(p) = \frac{1}{C_1'(x)} \qquad\qquad \text{for } p > \text{min A.V.C.}_1$$

and

6.2

$$\psi_1''(p) = \frac{1}{C_1''(x)} > 0 \qquad \text{for } p > \text{min A.V.C.}_1$$

The function $\psi_1(p)$ is strictly convex and is at least twice differentiable for all values of price in excess of minimum average variable cost. If $K_1 > 0$ and if $C_1'(x) > 0$ for all output values in excess of minimum average variable cost, then the function can be illustrated as in Figure 6.2. Similar conditions hold for the maximum profit function of technique two.

---

  [8] The same symbols are used for the maximum profit function as were used in the appendix to the previous chapter.

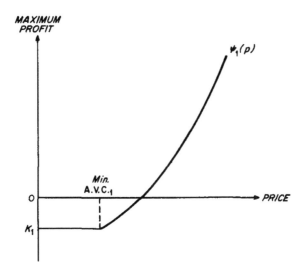

FIG. 6.2

The difference between these two maximum profit functions is

$$W(p) = \psi_1(p) - \psi_2(p). \qquad 6.3$$

To keep to the essentials of the analysis, let us consider only the properties of this function for price values in excess of the greatest of the minima of the average costs of the two techniques, i.e., for

$$p > \text{Max } \{\text{min A.V.C.}_1, \text{min A.V.C.}_2\}.$$

For these values of p,

$$W''(p) = \psi_1'' - \psi_2''$$

$$= \frac{1}{C_1''(x)} - \frac{1}{C_2''(x)} \qquad 6.4$$

For these values of p, the conditions for a maximum of profit require that $C_1''(x) > 0$ and $C_2''(x) > 0$ and, therefore, from equation 6.4,

$$W''(p) \gtreqless 0 \qquad 6.5$$

accordingly as

$$C_1''(x) \lesseqgtr C_2''(x). \qquad 6.6$$

If the price of the product is certain, i.e., if it is known in $t - n$ for t, and if the firm acts to maximize profit, the difference between the average profitability of the two techniques is

$$E[W(p)] = E[\psi_1(p)] - E[\psi_2(p)]. \qquad 6.7$$

If only the expected value of price is known in $t - n$ for t, if this expected value is stationary over time, and if the firm acts to maximize expected profit, the difference between the average profitability of the two techniques is

$$W(E[p]) = \psi_1(E[p]) - \psi_2(E[p]). \qquad 6.8$$

Taking a more particular case, if ρ_j represents the probability (relative frequency) of the jth possible price of the product, i.e., p_j, then under certainty the difference in the average profitability of the two techniques is

$$\sum_j \rho_j W(p_j) = \sum_j \rho_j \psi_1(p_j) - \sum_j \rho_j \psi_2(p_j) \qquad 6.9$$

and, under the above uncertainty conditions, this difference in profitability is

$$W\left(\sum_j \rho_j p_j\right) = \psi_1\left(\sum_j \rho_j p_j\right) - \psi_2\left(\sum_j \rho_j p_j\right). \qquad 6.10$$

If (i) $p > \text{Max } \{\text{Min A.V.C., Min A.V.C.}_2\}$, if (ii) all prices are not equal, if (iii) the same inequality relationship between $C_1''(x)$ and $C_2''(x)$ holds for all relevant values of output, and if (iv) the expected value of price under uncertainty equals the average value of price given certainty,

$$E[W(p)] \gtreqless W(E[p]) \qquad 6.11$$

accordingly as

$$C_1''(x) \lesseqgtr C_2''(x). \qquad 6.12$$

This is so because, from expressions 6.5 and 6.6, $W''(p) \gtreqqless 0$ accordingly as $C_1''(x) \lesseqqgtr C_2''(x)$. The relationship in 6.11 depends upon the convexity[9] of $W(p)$, which in turn depends upon the "relative" convexity of the techniques' cost functions. Taking a particular case, let ρ_j represent the relative frequency of the jth possible price of the product, and suppose that the above four conditions are satisfied, then

$$\sum_j \rho_j W(p_j) \gtreqqless W\left(\sum_j \rho_j p_j\right) \qquad 6.13$$

accordingly as

$$C_1''(x) \lesseqqgtr C_2''(x). \qquad 6.14$$

Under these conditions, the excess profitability of technique one under certainty is greater than, equal to, or less than that under uncertainty accordingly as the rate of change of marginal cost for technique one is less than, equal to, or greater than the rate of change of technique two's marginal cost. Given these circumstances, the relationship between expressions 6.11 and 6.12 implies that price uncertainty increases the excess average profitability of the technique with the *greatest* rate of change of marginal cost. It is implied that, if there is a change from one technique to another as a result of the occurrence of price uncertainty, it can, under the above conditions, be only away from the flexible technique and in favor of the inflexible technique.

This point can be illustrated by the example shown in Figure 6.3. In this figure, the function $W(p)$ is shown for $p > \text{Max}$ {Min A.V.C.$_1$, Min A.V.C.$_2$}. Two prices, p_1 and p_2, are assumed to be the only possible ones for the product, and $C_1''(x)$ is assumed to be less than $C_2''(x)$ for all relevant values of output. Technique one is more flexible than technique two. Consequently, $W''(p) > 0$ for the relevant domain of p-values; i.e., it is a strictly convex function. Under the assumed conditions

---

[9] For a proof of the relevant theorem concerning expectation of a variable dependent on a convex function, see G. H. Hardy, J. E. Littlewood, and G. Polya, *Inequalities*, Cambridge University Press, Cambridge, 1934, pp. 74–75, theorem 90.

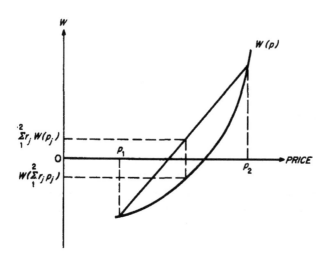

FIG. 6.3

of certainty, the excess average profitability of technique one is $\sum_{j=1}^{2}\rho_j W(p_j)$ and under the assumed conditions of uncertainty $W(\sum_{j=1}^{2}\rho_j p_j)$, where ρ_j represents the relative frequency of the jth possible price. If $p_1 \neq p_2$, it follows from the strict convexity of $W(p)$ that

$$\sum_{j=1}^{2}\rho_j W(p_j) > W(\sum_{j=1}^{2}\rho_j p_j). \qquad 6.15$$

Arbitrary values of ρ_j and p_j are used in Figure 6.3 to illustrate a case in which the excess average profitability of technique one, the flexible technique, is higher under certainty than under uncertainty. In the case illustrated, although technique one, the flexible technique, yields the greatest average profit under conditions of certainty of price, technique two, the inflexible technique, yields the greatest average profit under price uncertainty. The figure indicates that if a switch in techniques takes place as a result of price uncertainty, it will be in favor of the inflexible technique.

The point which emerges is that if there is no price which makes a shutdown of production optimal, then price uncertainty increases the probability of adoption of the inflexible production technique, i.e., the technique which has the greatest rate of change of marginal cost. The result does not accord with Baumol's hypothesis.

Relationships 6.11 and 6.12 also enable us to reach some conclusions about the influence of price instability upon technique choice. Suppose that price certainty exists. It then follows from these relationships that the excess average profitability of the technique which has the least rate of change of marginal cost is greater for a series of unstable prices than for a stable price equal to the average of the unstable prices. If certainty exists and the firm attempts to maximize average profit, increased price instability increases the likelihood that the firm will adopt the more flexible technique. This result accords with Stigler's hypothesis.

D. Model II—A Quadratic Cost Model which Makes a More General Allowance for Price Uncertainty

Assumptions (i), (ii), and (iii) limit the generality of the preceding model. To relax them, we shall, as in the second model of Chapter V, make the following assumptions:

(i) The firm's output in t equals its output planned for t in $t - n$.

(ii) The output of any period is independent of that of any other.

(iii) Costs are certain and stationary.

(iv) Total cost is quadratic.

(v) In addition, suppose that assumptions (iv), (v), (vi), and (vii) of the last model hold.

We do not suppose, as Marschak and Nelson[10] do, that

(i) the firm aims to maximize expected profit for each of the sub-periods of the techniques' length of life $T = \sum_{t=1}^{N} t$,

(ii) knows at the date of choosing its technique the relative frequency distribution of the "true" expected price values, and

(iii) knows at each production decision point the true expected price of the output dependent on that decision.

We shall suppose

(i) that the firm may adopt any combination of criteria or behavior pattern for the sub-periods of T but for its actual pattern for T it wishes to adopt the technique which yields the greatest average profit,[11] and

(ii) that at its technique decision date it holds an "anticipated" relative frequency distribution of actual prices and its shadow prices for T.

Assume that the firm is uncertain of the relative frequency distributions of the p and $\hat{p}$ which will occur over period T. If $E_e(\pi)$ represents the firm's decision value of average profit for T, e.g., the value which it feels is most likely, and if $E(\pi)$ represents its actual average profit given the actual p and $\hat{p}$ values of T,

$$\text{Prob } \{|E_e(\pi) - E(\pi)| > 0\} > 0.$$

However, I shall suppose that $E_e(\pi)$ is at least a monotonically increasing function of $E(\pi)$ or is very nearly so. More generally, I shall suppose that decision set values tend to vary in the same direction as actual values. Consequently, theorems will be

[10] Marschak and Nelson, *op. cit.*, pp. 42–58.
[11] This approach is made easier by the use of shadow prices.

developed in terms of *actual* p and $\hat{p}$ values applying the last model of Chapter V.

The profit functions of the two techniques, where subscripts represent the technique, can be represented for any sub-period as

$$\pi_i = px - (a_i x^2 + b_i x + c_i), \qquad (i = 1, 2). \qquad 6.16$$

By assumption, $a_i > 0$. From the argument used to derive equation 5.32, average profit of the alternative techniques is

$$E(\pi_i) = \frac{E(p)E(\hat{p}) + \text{cov}\,(p, \hat{p}) - b_i E(p)}{2a_i} - b_i \frac{E(\hat{p}) - b_i}{2a_i}$$

$$- \frac{E(\hat{p})^2 + \text{var}\,\hat{p} - 2b_i E(\hat{p}) + b_i{}^2}{4a_i} - c_i, \qquad (i = 1, 2).$$

$$6.17$$

Hence, from expression 6.17, we obtain the "excess" average profit from technique one, i.e.,

$$E[W] = E(\pi_1) - E(\pi_2), \qquad 6.18$$

in terms of the moments of shadow and actual prices, and a number of theorems follow.

If the average value of actual price $E(p)$ and the variance of price $\sigma_p{}^2$ are constant, then applying an argument similar to that used to obtain equation 5.35,

$$\Delta E[W] = -\left[\frac{1}{4a_1} - \frac{1}{4a_2}\right]\Delta M, \qquad 6.19$$

where, as before, M is a measure of price uncertainty, i.e., the mean of the squared deviations of actual from shadow price. Hence, if $E(p)$ and $\sigma_p{}^2$ are constant, then for an increase of M,

$$\Delta E[W] \gtreqless 0$$

accordingly as

$$2a_1 \gtreqless 2a_2.$$

Under these conditions, increased price uncertainty increases the probability of the firm's adoption of the most inflexible technique. The above inequalities imply that if the average value and variance of actual price are constant, then an increase in M increases the "excess" average profit of the technique which has the greatest rate of change of marginal cost.

Turn now to the influence of price instability upon the choice of a technique in this generalized setting. It can be shown that if M is constant and if $E(p)$ is constant, that an increase in the variance of price increases the likelihood that the firm will adopt the flexible technique. This, of course, includes the special case where price is certain, i.e., $M = 0$.

If $\Delta E(p) = 0$ and if $\Delta M = 0$, then, by extension of the argument which was used to derive equation 5.38,

$$\Delta E[W] = \left[\frac{1}{4a_1} - \frac{1}{4a_2} \right] \Delta \sigma_p^2. \qquad 6.20$$

Consequently, if $E(p)$ and M are constant, then, for an increase of the variance of price,

$$\Delta E[W] \gtreqless 0$$

accordingly as

$$2a_1 \lesseqgtr 2a_2.$$

It follows that increased price instability, price "uncertainty constant," raises the firm's probability of adopting the flexible technique. More accurately, if the average value of price and the mean square of deviations of shadow price from actual are constant, an increase of the variance of price raises the "excess" average profit of the technique which has the least rate of change of marginal cost and so increases its probability of adoption. We note that these results are in accordance with Stigler's hypothesis, since he may implicitly assume that $M = 0$.

Yet, we must be wary of this last hypothesis, since errors and price instability are not always independent. Circumstances can arise where increased price instability increases the likelihood that the more inflexible technique will be adopted rather than the flexible one. Let us maintain the symmetry of this argument with that of the last chapter by supposing that a regression line of p on $\hat{p}$ of

$$z = \gamma_0 + \gamma_1 \hat{p} \qquad\qquad 6.21$$

is maintained irrespective of which technique is chosen. Then, the need for caution becomes apparent, and we are able to show that Marschak and Nelson's model[12] is a special case of the one which is developed here. Now, the regression dependence of 6.21 limits the relationship of the moments in expression 6.18, and the specific form of $E[W]$ in this case is clear from equation 5.44. Since this is the case, there is no point in stating this rather long but straightforward expression for $E[W]$. We shall, however, use this specific form to state some theorems.

Consider the effect of price instability given these conditions. By extension of the argument used for deriving equation 5.46, if $\Delta R = 0$, if $\Delta E(p) = 0$, and if $\Delta E(\hat{p}) = 0$,

$$\Delta E[W] = \left[\frac{R^2(2\gamma_1 - 1)}{4a_1\gamma_1^2} - \frac{R^2(2\gamma_1 - 1)}{4a_2\gamma_1^2} \right] \Delta\sigma_p{}^2. \qquad 6.22$$

Hence, if $R \neq 0$ *and if* $\gamma_1 > 0.5$,

$$\frac{\partial E[W]}{\partial\sigma_p{}^2} \gtreqless 0$$

accordingly as

$$2a_1 \lesseqgtr 2a_2.$$

But, if $R \neq 0$ *and if* $\gamma_1 < 0.5$,

$$\frac{\partial E[W]}{\partial\sigma_p{}^2} \gtreqless 0$$

accordingly as

$$2a_1 \gtreqless 2a_2.$$

We see that, under these conditions, increased price instability increases the likelihood of adoption of the flexible technique

[12] Marschak and Nelson, *op. cit.*

if $\gamma_1 = R\sigma_p/\sigma_{\hat{p}} > 0.5$ *but* decreases this likelihood if $\gamma_1 < 0.5$. Therefore, any statement that increased price instability increases the likelihood of the adoption of a flexible technique needs to be qualified.

Again, under these circumstances, let us consider the effect upon technique choice of a change in R^2. Using the argument previously used to obtain equation 5.49, if $\Delta E(p) = 0$, if $\Delta E(\hat{p}) = 0$, and if $\Delta \sigma_p^2 = 0$, then, from equation 6.18,

$$\Delta E[W] = \left[\frac{\left(\dfrac{2}{\gamma_1} - \dfrac{1}{\gamma_1^2} \right)\sigma_p^2}{4a_1} - \frac{\left(\dfrac{2}{\gamma_1} - \dfrac{1}{\gamma_1^2} \right)\sigma_p^2}{4a_2} \right] \Delta R^2 \qquad 6.23$$

Hence, under these conditions, if $\sigma_p^2 \neq 0$ *and if* $\gamma_1 < 0.5$,

$$\frac{\partial E[W]}{\partial R^2} \gtrless 0$$

accordingly as

$$2a_1 \gtrless 2a_2.$$

But, if $\sigma_p^2 \neq 0$ *and if* $\gamma_1 > 0.5$,

$$\frac{\partial E[W]}{\partial R^2} \gtrless 0$$

accordingly as

$$2a_1 \lessgtr 2a_2.$$

We see that an increase in R^2 only favors the flexible technique if $\gamma_1 > 0.5$. If we take $1 - R^2$ as a measure of certainty, which I do not, an increase in price uncertainty increases the likelihood of adoption of the flexible technique if $\gamma_1 < 0.5$ but increases the likelihood of adoption of the inflexible technique if $\gamma_1 > 0.5$. If we take M as a measure of price uncertainty, which I do, then by extension of the result of equation 5.51, it remains true that the likelihood of adoption of the inflexible technique rises with M. The reasoning which surrounds equation 5.51 applies, *mutatis mutandis*.

It is of some interest to see how Marschak and Nelson's views on flexibility and technique choice fit into the preceding framework. They use Nelson's model which was mentioned in section F of the last chapter. This, as we saw previously, involves the assumption that $\hat{p}$ is an unbiased estimate of p, and specializes the regression of p on $\hat{p}$ to

$$z = \hat{p}. \qquad 6.24$$

Also, given that $E(p) = E(\hat{p})$, it specializes the restricted average profit function from the form of 5.44 to that of 5.53 and, consequently, it does the similar thing to the function $E[W]$. Hence, $E[W]$ assumes the special form

$$E[W] = \frac{R^2\sigma_p^2 + [E(p) - b_1]^2}{4a_1} - c_1$$

$$- \left\{ \frac{R^2\sigma_p^2 + [E(p) - b_2]^2}{4a_2} - c_2 \right\}. \qquad 6.25$$

If $R \neq 0$, $\dfrac{\partial E[W]}{\partial \sigma_p^2} = \dfrac{R^2}{4a_1} - \dfrac{R^2}{4a_2} \gtrless 0$

accordingly as

$$2a_1 \lessgtr 2a_2.$$

The relative "desirability" of the flexible plant is increased as price instability (as measured by the variance) increases, and this accords with our previous result, since in this case $\gamma_1 = 1$ and is, therefore, in excess of 0.5.

Also, in this particular case, if $\sigma_p^2 \neq 0$,

$$\frac{\partial E[W]}{\partial R^2} = \frac{\sigma_p^2}{4a_1} - \frac{\sigma_p^2}{4a_2} \gtrless 0$$

accordingly as

$$2a_1 \lessgtr 2a_2.$$

"The relative desirability of the flexible plant increases as ... the ability to predict market price before making an output decision increases." This again accords with our previous results, since in this special case $\gamma_1 = 1$. It also contradicts Baumol's hypothesis.

Marschak and Nelson's approach is an interesting one and fits into the previous framework as a special case. However, it might be remembered that in the more general case the relative desirability of the flexible plant is not necessarily increased by an increase in the variance of price or by an increase in R^2. Also, as was shown in Section F of Chapter V, M increases with $1 - R^2$ in Nelson's case, but this is not necessarily so in the general linear regression case.

E. Conclusion

There is always some danger that logical details will block out the main drift of an argument such as the one above. Therefore, leaving the details aside, the analysis suggests that increased price uncertainty increases the likelihood of adoption of inflexible techniques. On the other hand, while increased price instability increases the likelihood of adoption of flexible techniques if price is certain or if "price uncertainty is constant," it does not do so in all circumstances. Even if the coefficient of correlation is positive, increased, price instability need not favor the flexible technique.

The analysis shows some theories to be special cases and to be misleading or in need of qualification. In particular, the view that increased price uncertainty favors the flexible technique seems erroneous. Throughout, the flexibility of a technique has been defined in terms of the rate of change of marginal cost. The static decision-making assumption of no divergence of actual output from "planned" has ruled out flexibility in Hart's sense. The next chapter provides us with an opportunity to relax this assumption and take account of flexibility in Hart's sense.

CHAPTER VII

Dynamic Decision-Making,
Average Profit,
and Technique Choice

A. Introduction

The analysis up to this stage has been based upon the static decision-making assumption of no divergence of actual output from "planned," and it has, therefore, ruled out flexibility in Hart's sense.[1] It is the purpose of this chapter to allow for a divergence of actual output from "planned" at a cost and to trace through the implications of this possibility for average profit and technique choice.

To some extent, this development includes the previous one as a special case, since the former decision-making case can be considered as one in which the costs of divergence from plan are so high that divergence is not worthwhile. Under this extended set of circumstances, the previous hypotheses about average profit and technique choice continue to hold; e.g., it is still true that even if the coefficient of linear correlation of shadow and actual prices is positive and constant, increased price instability can decrease average profit. We can also take account of flexibility in Hart's sense showing that, other things equal, "increased price uncertainty," increases the probability of the firm's adopting the technique with the least rate of change of the marginal cost of divergence of actual output from "planned."

B. Average Profit

The aim is to extend the analysis but to retain simplicity at the same time. This can be done by concentrating on quad-

[1] A. G. Hart, "Risk, Uncertainty, and the Unprofitability of Compounding Probabilities," pp. 110–118 in *Studies in Mathematical Economics and Econometrics*, O. Lange, F. McIntyre, and F. Yntema, eds., The University of Chicago Press, Chicago, 1942.

ratic cost functions and making some special dependence assumptions. We shall use the following assumptions:

(i) The firm makes only two decisions upon its output for any period t. The first is made in period $t - n$, $n \geq 1$, and the second is made in period t when the actual price value is known. For any given output, costs may be increased by a difference between the first and second decision.

(ii) The planned outputs (and their associated costs) are independent and so also are the actual outputs (and costs) of different periods.

(iii) The total cost function of any period is stationary and is known.

(iv) For any period, where x^* represents the output which is planned for the period and x represents the actual output for the period, this cost function is of the form

$$C = \sum_{i=0}^{2} a_i x^i + \sum_{i=0}^{2} b_i (x - x^*)^i \qquad 7.1$$

where $a_2 > 0$, $b_2 \geq 0$, and $b_0 \geq 0$ according as $|x - x^*| \geq 0$.

Because the above cost function is quadratic, profit can be expressed as a quadratic function of actual and shadow prices. Consequently, expected profit can be expressed as a linear function of the first two moments of actual and shadow prices. Also, the principle of certainty equivalence[2] applies because this function is quadratic in the uncontrolled variable p, which represents the actual price of the product.

To reduce the algebra without changing the essence of the

[2] See, for the development of the principles of certainty equivalence, H. Theil, "Econometric Models and Welfare Maximization," *Weltwirtschaftliches Archiv*, vol. 72 (1954), pp. 60–83; H. Theil, "Note on Certainty Equivalence in Dynamic Economic Planning," *Econometrica*, vol. 25 (1957), pp. 346–349; H. A. Simon, "Dynamic Programming under Uncertainty with a Quadratic Criterion Function," *Econometrica*, vol. 24 (1956), pp. 74–81.

argument, let us consider a special form of 7.1. Assume a cost function of the form,

$$C(x, x^*) = \alpha_0 + \alpha_1 x^2 + \alpha_2 (x - x^*)^2, \qquad 7.2$$

where $\alpha_0 \geq 0$, $\alpha_1 > 0$, $\alpha_2 \geq 0$. The firm's profit function for any period is then

$$\pi = px - \{\alpha_0 + \alpha_1 x^2 + \alpha_2 x^2 - 2\alpha_2 x x^* + \alpha_2 x^{*2}\}. \qquad 7.3$$

Now, whatever value of x^* is chosen in $t - n$, the firm "should" always choose x in t so as to maximize profit given x^*. The final decision in t must be optimal whatever value of x^* happens to have been chosen in $t - n$.[3] A necessary condition for a maximum of profit with respect to x is that

$$\frac{\partial \pi}{\partial x} = 0 \qquad 7.4$$

which requires

$$x = \frac{p + 2\alpha_2 x^*}{2\alpha_1 + 2\alpha_2}. \qquad 7.5$$

For $x \geq 0$, 7.5 gives the value of x which maximizes profit. Substituting 7.5 into equation 7.3, we obtain an expression which is quadratic in p.

It is now possible to pose the problem of what value of x^* should be chosen in $t - n$ *given* some probability distribution of p-values for period t and supposing that output in t will always be such as to maximize profit *given* x^*. If the firm wishes to maximize expected profit, it can do this by setting

$$x^* = \frac{E(p)}{2\alpha_1}, \qquad 7.6$$

[3] The principle involved here has been fruitfully used by R. Bellman in dynamic programming. See R. E. Bellman and S. E. Dreyfus, *Applied Dynamic Programming*, Princeton University Press, Princeton, 1962. They state the principle, on page 15, in the following terms: "The Principle of Optimality. An optimal policy has the property that whatever the initial state and the initial decision are, the remaining decisions must constitute an optimal policy with regard to the state resulting from the first decision."

where $E(p)$ is the expected value of price for the given probability distribution of price. This result is obtained by substituting equation 7.5 into 7.3. In the resulting expression Z, x^* is a controlled variable and p is uncontrolled. Since Z is quadratic in p, to maximize its expected value with respect to x^* we can substitute $E(p)$ in place of p and maximize this expression ξ. Doing so, we find that the equality of 7.6 is a necessary condition for a maximum of $E[Z]$. The substitution of $E(p)$ for p is permissible in this case because Z is a quadratic function in p, the principle of certainty equivalence holds,[4] and the expressions ξ and $E[Z]$ differ only by a constant.[5] The value of x^* which maximizes ξ also maximizes $E[Z]$.

However, the analysis is not primarily concerned with optimality but rather with the effect upon average profit of price uncertainty and instability under a wide range of behavioral possibilities. Whatever the non-negative value of x^*, there will be a value of $\hat{p}$ such that

$$x^* = \frac{\hat{p}}{2\alpha_1},$$
7.7

and if we set p equal to this value and maximize function 7.3, we will obtain the actual value of x^*. Also, if profit is to be maximized whatever value of x^* is chosen,

$$x = \frac{p + 2\alpha_2 x^*}{2\alpha_1 + 2\alpha_2}$$

$$= \frac{p + \dfrac{2\alpha_2}{2\alpha_1}\hat{p}}{2\alpha_1 + 2\alpha_2}.$$
7.8

[4] See Theil, *op. cit.*; Simon, *op. cit.*
[5] Cf. H. Theil, "Some Reflections on Static Programming under Uncertainty," *Weltwirtschaftliches Archiv*, vol. 87 (1961), pp. 124–138, esp. pp. 128–129.

Consequently, after expressions 7.7 and 7.8 are substituted into equation 7.3, average profit becomes the following function of actual and shadow prices:

$$E(\pi) = E\left\{p\left(\frac{p + \dfrac{2\alpha_2}{2\alpha_1}\hat{p}}{2\alpha_1 + 2\alpha_2}\right) - \alpha_0 - (\alpha_1 + \alpha_2)\left(\frac{p + \dfrac{2\alpha_2}{2\alpha_1}\hat{p}}{2\alpha_1 + 2\alpha_2}\right)^2\right.$$

$$\left. + \frac{2\alpha_2}{2\alpha_1}\hat{p}\left(\frac{p + \dfrac{2\alpha_2}{2\alpha_1}\hat{p}}{2\alpha_1 + 2\alpha_2}\right) - \alpha_2\left(\frac{\hat{p}}{2\alpha_1}\right)^2\right\} \qquad 7.9$$

$$= \frac{1}{4\alpha_1 + 4\alpha_2}\left[E(p)^2 + \operatorname{var} p + \frac{2\alpha_2}{2\alpha_1}[2E(p)E(\hat{p}) + 2\operatorname{cov}(p, \hat{p})]\right.$$

$$\left. - \frac{2\alpha_2}{2\alpha_1}[E(\hat{p})^2 + \operatorname{var}\hat{p}]\right] - \alpha_0. \qquad 7.10[6]$$

[6] To derive equation 7.10 we express equation 7.9 as

$$E(\pi) = \frac{E(p)^2 + \operatorname{var} p + \dfrac{2\alpha_2}{2\alpha_1}[E(p)E(\hat{p}) + \operatorname{cov}(p, \hat{p})]}{2\alpha_1 + 2\alpha_2} - \alpha_0$$

$$- \frac{E(p)^2 + \operatorname{var} p + \dfrac{4\alpha_2}{2\alpha_1}[E(p)E(\hat{p}) + \operatorname{cov}(p, \hat{p})] + \dfrac{4\alpha_2^2}{4\alpha_1^2}[E(\hat{p})^2 + \operatorname{var}\hat{p}]}{4\alpha_1 + 4\alpha_2}$$

$$+ \frac{\dfrac{2\alpha_2}{2\alpha_1}[E(p)E(\hat{p}) + \operatorname{cov}(p, \hat{p})] + \dfrac{4\alpha_2^2}{4\alpha_1^2}[E(\hat{p})^2 + \operatorname{var}\hat{p}]}{2\alpha_1 + 2\alpha_2}$$

$$- \frac{\alpha_2[E(\hat{p})^2 + \operatorname{var}\hat{p}]}{4\alpha_1^2} \qquad (i)$$

$$= \frac{E(p)^2 + \operatorname{var} p + \dfrac{4\alpha_2}{2\alpha_1}[E(p)E(\hat{p}) + \operatorname{cov}(p, \hat{p})] + \dfrac{4\alpha_2^2}{4\alpha_1^2}[E(\hat{p})^2 + \operatorname{var} p]}{4\alpha_1 + 4\alpha_2}$$

$$- \frac{\alpha_2[E(\hat{p})^2 + \operatorname{var}\hat{p}]}{4\alpha_1^2} - \alpha_0 \qquad (ii)$$

Multiplying the last term of (ii) by $\left(\dfrac{1}{\alpha_1} + \dfrac{\alpha_2}{\alpha_1^2}\right) \Big/ \left(\dfrac{1}{\alpha_1} + \dfrac{\alpha_2}{\alpha_1^2}\right)$

and collecting terms, we obtain equation 7.10.

Equation 7.10 enables us to derive a number of theorems about the effect of price uncertainty and instability upon average profit and to extend the results to technique choice. First, consider the effect of increased price uncertainty upon average profit, assuming that the average value of price and the variance of price are constant. If $\Delta E(p) = 0$ and $\Delta \text{var}\, p = 0$, then, from equation 7.10,

$$\Delta E(\pi) = \frac{2\alpha_2/2\alpha_1}{4\alpha_1 + 4\alpha_2} \{[2E(p) - 2E(\hat{p})]\Delta E(\hat{p})$$

$$+ 2\Delta\text{cov}(p, \hat{p}) - \text{var}\, \hat{p}\} \qquad 7.11$$

$$= -\frac{2\alpha_2/2\alpha_1}{2(2\alpha_1 + 2\alpha_2)} \Delta M \qquad 7.12$$

$$= \left[\frac{1}{2(2\alpha_1 + 2\alpha_2)} - \frac{1}{4\alpha_1}\right] \Delta M \qquad 7.13$$

where[7] ΔM represents the change of the mean of squared deviations of shadow from actual price. The substitution of ΔM in equation 7.11 is possible since, from 5.34, if $\Delta E(p) = 0$ and if $\Delta \sigma_p{}^2 = 0$,

$$\Delta M = [-2E(p) + 2E(\hat{p})]\Delta E(\hat{p}) - 2\,\text{cov}\,(p, \hat{p}) + \Delta \sigma_{\hat{p}}{}^2.$$

[7] The coefficient of equation 7.13 is obtained as follows:

$$\frac{2\alpha_2/2\alpha_1}{4\alpha_1 + 4\alpha_2} = \frac{\alpha_2}{4\alpha_2\alpha_1 + 4\alpha_1{}^2}. \qquad \text{(i)}$$

$$\frac{1 + (2\alpha_1/2\alpha_2)}{2(2\alpha_1 + 2\alpha_2)} = \frac{\alpha_1 + \alpha_2}{4\alpha_2\alpha_1 + 4\alpha_1{}^2} \qquad \text{(ii)}$$

$$= \frac{1}{4\alpha_1}. \qquad \text{(iii)}$$

Therefore,

$$\frac{2\alpha_2/2\alpha_1}{4\alpha_1 + 4\alpha_2} = \frac{1}{4\alpha_1} - \frac{\alpha_1}{4\alpha_1(\alpha_1 + \alpha_2)}$$

$$= \frac{1}{4\alpha_1} - \frac{1}{2(2\alpha_1 + 2\alpha_2)}. \qquad \text{(iv)}$$

It follows from equation 7.13 that if $E(p)$ and var p are constant, if $2\alpha_2 > 0$, and if $0 < 2\alpha_1 < \infty$,

$$E(\pi) \gtreqless 0$$

accordingly as

$$\Delta M \lesseqgtr 0.$$

If the rate of change of the marginal cost of divergence from plan is positive,[8] increased price uncertainty reduces average profit. Specifically, if average price and the variance of price are constant, an increase in M decreases average profit by ΔM times the reciprocal of twice the rate of change of the marginal cost of "output" less the reciprocal of twice the rate of change of the marginal cost of optimally planned output. The reduction of average profit is greater, the greater the rate of change of the marginal cost of divergence of actual output from "planned."

Turning now to the influence of price variability, suppose that as the variability of price changes, M, the degree of uncertainty, remains constant. If $E(p)$ alone is necessarily constant, it follows from equation 7.10 that

$$\Delta E(\pi)$$
$$= \frac{\Delta\sigma_p{}^2 + \dfrac{2\alpha_2}{2\alpha_1}\{[2E(p) - 2E(\hat{p})]\Delta E(\hat{p}) + 2\Delta\mathrm{cov}(p,\hat{p}) - \Delta\sigma_{\hat{p}}{}^2\}}{4\alpha_1 + 4\alpha_2}$$

$$7.14$$

But, since ΔM is assumed to be equal to zero in this case, it follows from equation 5.34 that

$$[-2E(p) + 2E(p)]\Delta E(\hat{p}) - 2\,\mathrm{cov}(p, \hat{p}) + \Delta\sigma_{\hat{p}}{}^2 = -\Delta\sigma_p{}^2.$$

$$7.15$$

Consequently, if we multiply 7.15 by -1, we may substitute in 7.14 and obtain the change of average profit for a change in

---

[8] If $2\alpha_2 = 0$ and if $E(p)$ and $\sigma_p{}^2$ are constant, then, from equation 7.13, increases in M do not change $E(\pi)$. In this case, increased errors leave expected profit unchanged.

the variability of price, average price and the degree of price uncertainty being assumed constant. We obtain

$$\Delta E(\pi) = \frac{1 + (2\alpha_2/2\alpha_1)}{2(2\alpha_1 + 2\alpha_2)} \Delta \text{ var } p \qquad 7.16$$

$$= \frac{1}{4\alpha_1} \Delta \text{ var } p. \qquad 7.17$$

The reduction of the coefficient of Δvar p is shown in footnote 7 of this chapter.

It follows from equation 7.17 that if $\Delta E(p) = 0$, if $\Delta M = 0$, and if $0 < 2\alpha_1 < \infty$, that

$$\Delta E(\pi) \gtreqless 0$$

accordingly as

$$\Delta \text{ var } p \gtreqless 0.$$

If price uncertainty and the average value of price are constant, increased price instability increases average profit. Specifically, if M and average price are constant, an increase in the variance of price increases average profit by the reciprocal of twice the rate of change of the marginal cost of optimally planned output times the rise in the price variance's value. Again, in the special case where price is certain, $M = 0$, and, therefore, increased price instability raises average profit in this particular case.

C. Regression Restrictions on the Moments of the Average Profit Function

It is of interest to consider, along the same lines as in Chapter V, the restrictions which a linear regression relationship of the p and $\hat{p}$ values place upon the moments of equation 7.10. After doing this and allowing for divergence from plan, it is possible to show that even if the linear correlation coefficient of prices and shadow prices is positive, increased price instability can decrease average profit.

Assume that the "population" regression of p on $\hat{p}$ is

$$z = \gamma_0 + \gamma_1 \hat{p}$$

and that this regression is maintained. Then, as before,

$$\sigma_{\hat{p}}^2 = \frac{R^2 \sigma_p^2}{\gamma_1^2}$$

and

$$\text{cov}\,(p,\hat{p}) = \frac{R^2 \sigma_p^2}{\gamma_1}.$$

Substituting these values into equation 7.10, we obtain

$$E(\pi) = \frac{E(p)^2 + \sigma_p^2 + \dfrac{2\alpha_2}{2\alpha_1} \times \left\{ 2E(p)E(\hat{p}) + \dfrac{2R^2}{\gamma_1}\sigma_p^2 - E(\hat{p})^2 - \dfrac{R^2}{\gamma_1^2}\sigma_p^2 \right\}}{4\alpha_1 + 4\alpha_2} - \alpha_0.$$

$$7.18$$

Given equation 7.18, consider the effect upon average profit of an increase in the variance of price if the average values of price and of shadow price are constant. From equation 7.18,

$$\frac{\partial E(\pi)}{\partial \sigma_p^2} = \frac{1 + \dfrac{2\alpha_2}{2\alpha_1}\left[\dfrac{2R^2}{\gamma_1} - \dfrac{R^2}{\gamma_1^2}\right]}{2(2\alpha_1 + 2\alpha_2)}. \qquad 7.19$$

Since

$$\gamma_1 = \frac{R\sigma_p}{\sigma_{\hat{p}}},$$

equation 7.19 can be expressed as

$$\frac{\partial E(\pi)}{\partial \sigma_p^2} = \frac{1 + \dfrac{2\alpha_2\sigma_{\hat{p}}}{2\alpha_1\sigma_p}\left[2R - \dfrac{\sigma_{\hat{p}}}{\sigma_p}\right]}{2(2\alpha_1 + 2\alpha_2)}. \qquad 7.20$$

If $\sigma_{\hat{p}} > 2R\sigma_p$ and if $2\alpha_2\sigma_{\hat{p}}/2\alpha_1\sigma_p$ is large enough, $\partial E(\pi)/\partial \sigma_p^2$ will be negative. *It can clearly be negative even if $R > 0$.* It is more likely to be negative the greater the ratio of the rate of change of the marginal cost of divergence to the rate of change of marginal cost of optimally planned output. Our result conflicts with Oi's hypothesis;[9] in this dynamic decision-making case, even if $R > 0$, increased price variability need not increase expected profit. However, if $2\alpha_2 = 0$ and if $0 < 2\alpha_1 < \infty$, an increase in the variance of price increases average profit. The increase is the same as if price certainty existed, and the value of M is immaterial for average profit.

It is of interest also to follow up the particular case where shadow prices are unbiased estimates of actual price. The linear regression equation

$$z = \gamma_0 + \gamma_1 \hat{p}$$

specializes to

$$z = \hat{p}, \qquad 7.21$$

and in this case $E(p) = E(\hat{p})$. Consequently, the expected profit function, 7.18, further specializes to[10]

$$E(\pi) = \frac{E(p)^2 + \dfrac{2\alpha_2}{2\alpha_1} E(p)^2 + \sigma_p{}^2 + \dfrac{2\alpha_2}{2\alpha_1} R^2 \sigma_p{}^2}{4\alpha_1 + 4\alpha_2} \qquad 7.22$$

$$= \frac{1}{4\alpha_1} E(p)^2 + \frac{1}{2(2\alpha_1 + 2\alpha_2)} (1 - R^2)\sigma_p{}^2 + \frac{1}{4\alpha_1} R^2 \sigma_p{}^2. \qquad 7.23$$

---

[9] W. Oi, "Rejoinder," *Econometrica*, Vol. 31, 1963, p. 248.

[10] We obtain the coefficients of $\sigma_p{}^2$ in equation 7.23 as follows:

The coefficient of $\sigma_p{}^2$ in equation 7.22 is

$$\frac{1 + (2\alpha_2/2\alpha_1)R^2}{2(2\alpha_1 + 2\alpha_2)} = \frac{1}{2(2\alpha_1 + 2\alpha_2)} + \frac{2\alpha_2/2\alpha_1}{4\alpha_1 + 4\alpha_2} R^2 \qquad (i)$$

$$= \frac{1}{2(2\alpha_1 + 2\alpha_2)} - \frac{1}{2(2\alpha_1 + 2\alpha_2)} R^2 + \frac{1}{4\alpha_1} R^2 \qquad (ii)$$

$$= \frac{1}{2(2\alpha_1 + 2\alpha_2)} (1 - R^2) + \frac{1}{4\alpha_1} R^2. \qquad (iii)$$

To obtain (ii), we use the results of footnote 7 of this chapter.

Taking this particular model, let us examine the effect upon average profit of an increase in price uncertainty. If the average value of price and the variance of price are constant, then, from equation 7.23,

$$\frac{\partial E(\pi)}{\partial(1 - R^2)} = \left[\frac{1}{2(2\alpha_1 + 2\alpha_2)} - \frac{1}{4\alpha_1}\right]\sigma_p^2. \qquad 7.24$$

Therefore, if the rate of change of the marginal cost of divergence from plan exceeds zero, i.e., if $2\alpha_2 > 0$, if $\sigma_p^2 > 0$, and if $0 < 2\alpha_1 < \infty$,

$$\frac{\partial E(\pi)}{\partial(1 - R^2)} < 0. \qquad 7.25$$

An increase in $1 - R^2$, or a decrease in the coefficient of linear correlation, decreases average profit if the above conditions apply. In these circumstances,[11] M increases with increases of $1 - R^2$. If the rate of change of the marginal cost of divergence from plan is zero, i.e., if $2\alpha_2 = 0$,

$$\frac{\partial E(\pi)}{\partial(1 - R^2)} = 0$$

and increased price uncertainty does not affect average profit.

Next, let us take account of the influence of increased price variability upon average profit if this particular model applies. If $E(p)$ and R^2 are constant, then, from equation 7.23,

$$\frac{\partial E(\pi)}{\partial \sigma_p^2} = \frac{1}{2(2\alpha_1 + 2\alpha_2)}(1 - R^2) + \frac{1}{4\alpha_1}R^2 \qquad 7.26$$

and, therefore, if $R^2 > 0$ and if $0 < 2\alpha_1 < \infty$,

$$\frac{\partial E(\pi)}{\partial \sigma_p^2} > 0.$$

Under these circumstances, if the average value of price is constant and if the correlation coefficient is positive, increased price variability, as measured by the price variance,

---

[11] Consider the discussion below equation 5.55.

increases average profit. However, if the linear regression of p on $\hat{p}$ is not restricted to the particular case where $\gamma_0 = 0$ and $\gamma_1 = 1$, a positive R-value is no guarantee that increased price instability increases average profit.

The results so far leave the broad conclusions of Chapter V unaltered. Allowing for minor qualifications, a number of broad "generalizations" have emerged. Without being specific, let us state some of them. If the rate of change of the marginal cost of divergence from plan is positive, increased price uncertainty reduces average profit. Also, if "price uncertainty" is constant, increased price variability increases the firm's average profit. However, if the linear regression of p on $\hat{p}$ is unchanging, increased price instability need not increase average profit even if the linear correlation coefficient is positive. The qualifications, which ensure these conclusions, have been stated above.

D. Technique Choice

Using the above analysis, we can now extend our discussion of the effects of price uncertainty and instability upon the choice of techniques. In Chapter VI, the firm's actual output was assumed not to diverge from "planned," and this ruled out flexibility in Hart's sense. Account can now be taken of flexibility in Hart's sense. Suppose that

(i) the firm has a choice of a technique A or B for period T consisting of N sub-periods,
(ii) the techniques have equal resale (scrap) value at the end of T, and
(iii) the production conditions which were previously outlined in this chapter hold.

The excess average profit of technique A is then

$$E[W] = E(\pi_A) - E(\pi_B) \qquad 7.27$$

where $E(\pi_A)$ and $E(\pi_B)$ are of similar form to equation 7.10.

Consider the influence of increased price uncertainty upon technique choice. It follows from equation 7.12 that, if the average value and variance of price are constant, an increase in M changes the "excess" average profit of technique A by

$$\Delta E[W] = \left[-\frac{2\alpha_{2,A}/2\alpha_{1,A}}{2(2\alpha_{1,A} + 2\alpha_{2,A})} + \frac{2\alpha_{2,B}/2\alpha_{1,B}}{2(2\alpha_{1,B} + 2\alpha_{2,B})} \right] \Delta M. \quad 7.28$$

This equation can also be expressed in the form of equation 7.13. Assuming that none of the rates of change of marginal cost is zero or infinite, it follows from expression 7.28 that if $\Delta E(p) = 0$, if $\Delta \sigma_p{}^2 = 0$, and if $\Delta M > 0$, then, if $2\alpha_{2,A} = 2\alpha_{2,B}$,

$$\Delta E[W] \gtreqless 0$$

accordingly as

$$2\alpha_{1,A} \gtreqless 2\alpha_{1,B}.$$

Under similar conditions, if $2\alpha_{1,A} = 2\alpha_{1,B}$, then

$$\Delta E[W] \gtreqless 0$$

accordingly as

$$2\alpha_{2,A} \lesseqgtr 2\alpha_{2,B}.$$

Under these conditions, if the rate of change of the marginal cost of the divergence of output from "planned" is the same for both techniques, an increase in M increases the likelihood of the firm's adopting the technique which has the greatest rate of change of marginal cost of optimally planned output. Also, if the rate of change of optimally planned output is the same for both techniques, an increase in M increases the probability of the firm's adopting the technique which has the least rate of change of the marginal cost of divergence from plan. Broadly, if average price and the variance of price are constant, an increase in M increases the probability of the firm's adoption of any technique which has both the greatest rate of change of marginal cost of optimally planned output and the lowest rate of change of the marginal cost of divergence from plan. While it is true that increased price uncertainty tends to favor the flexible technique, taking Hart's view of flexibility, it favors the inflexible technique if Baumol's "definition" of flexibility is adopted.

Next, let us deal with the general influence of price instability upon technique choice. If average price and M are constant, it follows, by application of the result of equation 7.17, that

$$\Delta E[W] = \left| \frac{1}{4\alpha_{1,A}} - \frac{1}{4\alpha_{1,B}} \right| \Delta \operatorname{var} p. \qquad 7.29$$

Therefore, under these conditions,

$$\Delta E[W] \gtreqless 0$$

accordingly as

$$2\alpha_{1,A} \lesseqgtr 2\alpha_{1,B}.$$

Consequently, if $E(p)$ and M are constant, an increase in the price variance increases the probability of the firm's adoption of the technique which has the lowest rate of change of marginal cost of "optimally planned" output. The more flexible technique, given Stigler's apparent usage, is favored by increased price variability if "price uncertainty" is constant.

Let us give some attention to the particular case in which the $\hat{p}$ values are unbiased estimates of p. $E(\pi_A)$ and $E(\pi_B)$ then assume the special form of equation 7.22. We observe from equation 7.24 that if $E(p)$ and σ_p^2 are constant, and if $\sigma_p^2 > 0$, that $[\partial E(\pi)/\partial E(1 - R^2)]$ is less negative the greater $2\alpha_1$, and the smaller $2\alpha_2$. Consequently, in these circumstances, an increase in $1 - R^2$ increases the probability of the firm's adoption of any technique which has the greatest rate of change of marginal cost of optimally planned output and the lowest rate of change of marginal cost of divergence from plan.

Continuing to suppose that the $\hat{p}$-values are unbiased estimates of p, if $E(p)$ and R^2 are constant and $R \neq 1$, it follows from equation 7.26 that $[\partial E(\pi)/\partial \sigma_p^2]$ is more positive the smaller $2\alpha_1$ and $2\alpha_2$. It follows, then, that in this case an increase of the price variance increases the probability of the firm's adoption of the technique which has the least rate of change of the marginal cost of optimally planned output and the least rate of change of the marginal cost of divergence from plan. We note that if $R = 0$ in this dynamic decision-making case increased price instability can influence technique choice, whereas it does not in the static decision-making case if $R = 0$.

Generally, it seems that increased price uncertainty favors the technique which involves the least rate of change of marginal cost of divergence from plan and the greatest rate of change of the marginal cost of "optimally planned" output. Increased price variability, "price uncertainty constant," favors the technique which has the least rate of change of marginal cost of optimally planned output. If price variability affects errors, it may favor techniques with the least rate of change of the marginal cost of divergence from plan and the greatest rate of change of the marginal cost of "optimally planned output." Our general results do not contradict the conclusions of Chapter VI.

E. Conclusion

The results of this chapter accord with the conclusions of Chapters V and VI. If the rate of change of the marginal cost of divergence from plan is positive, increased price uncertainty reduces the firm's average profit, and increased price instability may, but does not necessarily, raise average profit. This is so even if the linear correlation coefficient of actual and shadow price is positive. As for technique choice, increased price uncertainty favors techniques with the least rate of change of the marginal cost of divergence from plan and the *greatest* rate of change of marginal cost of optimally planned output. If "price uncertainty" is constant, increased price variability tends to favor techniques which have the *least* rate of change of marginal cost. But there is no guarantee that "price uncertainty" will be unaffected by price variability, and, therefore, some qualification is necessary about the general influence of increased price instability upon technique choice.

CHAPTER VIII

Price Uncertainty and
Industry Profit

A. Introduction

In economics, central importance has always been attached to the implications of individual actions for group or social outcomes, and so far this analysis has concentrated on the position of the individual firm. This development can, of course, be defended since we have not dealt with isolated incidents but with factors which affect all firms. But we can extend our analysis, and we shall do so in this chapter by taking account of the influence of price uncertainty on industry profit.

Before doing so, we might note some important general views of F. H. Knight[1] upon the subject of profit. In Knight's view, profit arises from the presence of uncertainty, i.e., the presence of "uninsurable risks." Assuming that profit is zero under certainty, he suggests that "profit arises from the fact that entrepreneurs contract for productive services in advance at fixed rates, and realize upon their use by the sale of the product in the market after it is made. Thus the competition for productive services is based upon anticipations. The prices of the productive services being the costs of production, changes in conditions give rise to profit by upsetting anticipations and producing a divergence between costs and selling price, which would be equalized by competition."[2]

Knight also maintains the following position: "The condition, then, under which entrepreneurs as a group will realize a profit is that they *underestimate* the prospects of their business relatively to their dispositions to venture. If, on the contrary, they *overestimate* their prospects (considering the degree of

[1] F. H. Knight, *Risk, Uncertainty, and Profit*, Houghton Mifflin Company, New York, 1921.
[2] *Ibid.*, pp. 197–198.

conviction necessary to move their wills) they will in aggregate suffer loss, and if they estimate correctly on the whole neither will occur. If the estimates are a matter of pure chance it would seem that the variations in the two directions would be equal, the average correct and the general level of profit zero."[3]

A formulation is introduced below which enables us to consider Knight's views and introduce some additional theorems about the influence of price uncertainty on industry profit. The formulation suggests that some of Knight's propositions need modification. It indicates that increased price uncertainty does reduce the industry's expected profit under a wide range of conditions.

B. Formulation of the Influence
of Price Uncertainty on Industry Profit

This formulation assumes static decision-making by firms' but it can be regarded as a simple approximation for cases where firms may diverge from plans at additional cost. The following assumptions are made:

    (i) Each firm in the industry makes one product.

   (ii) The industry is "closed" with k firms in it.

  (iii) No firm's output in t can diverge from the output "planned" for t in $t - n$.

  (iv) The only dependence in production occurs between the "plans" of $t - n$ and the output n periods later.

   (v) Each individual firm's marginal cost is a linear and increasing function of its output and all cost functions are identical.

  (vi) The demand function is a linear decreasing one of the industry's output equals sales.

 (vii) Cost and demand functions do not vary with time.

These assumptions are more particular than are required for our conclusions but greatly simplify the formal analysis.

---

[3] *Ibid.*, pp. 363–364.

Formalizing, let X represent the aggregate output of the industry in any sub-period, and let x_i represent the output of the ith firm in the same period. Then,

$$X = \sum_{i=1}^{k} x_i.$$

Let

$$P(X) = \beta_0 - \beta_1 X \qquad\qquad 8.1$$

represent the industry's demand function for any sub-period where $P(X)$ represents the demand price. Then, where

$$C_i = ax_i^2 + bx_i + c, \qquad a > 0, b \gtreqless 0, \qquad 8.2$$

represents the cost of the ith firm, industry profit in any period is

$$\Pi = \beta_0 X - \beta_1 X^2 - \sum_{i=1}^{k} (ax_i^2 + bx_i + c). \qquad 8.3$$

In any period, represent the average output per firm in the industry by μ_x, i.e.,

$$\mu_x = \frac{1}{k} \sum_{i=1}^{k} x_i = \frac{X}{k} \qquad\qquad 8.4$$

and represent the variance of the output between firms by σ_x^2, i.e.,

$$\sigma_x^2 = \frac{1}{k} \sum_{i=1}^{k} (\mu_x - x_i)^2. \qquad\qquad 8.5$$

Then industry's profit for any period, i.e., equation 8.3, can be expressed in the following convenient form:

$$\Pi = \beta_0 X - \beta_1 X^2 - k \left[\frac{\Sigma C_i}{k} \right]$$

$$= \beta_0 X - \beta_1 X^2 - k[a\mu_x^2 + a\sigma_x^2 + b\mu_x + c]$$

$$= \beta_0 X - \beta_1 X^2 - \frac{a}{k} X^2 - ka\sigma_x^2 - bX - kc. \qquad 8.6$$

Hence, if X is treated as a random variable or if we interpret $E(\Pi)$ as an average value over time, i.e., as $\dfrac{1}{N} \sum\limits_{t=1}^{N} \Pi_t$, and treat the other moments appropriately, expected profit or average profit for the industry is

$$E(\Pi) = \beta_0 E(X) - \beta_1 E(X)^2 - \beta_1 \text{ var } X - \frac{a}{k} E(X)^2$$

$$- \frac{a}{k} \text{ var } X - E(ka\sigma_x^2) - bE(X) - kc. \qquad 8.7$$

Consequently,

$$\frac{\partial E(\Pi)}{\partial \text{ var } X} = -\beta_1 - \frac{a}{k} < 0. \qquad 8.8$$

If other things are constant, an increase in the variance of the industry's output reduces the average profit of the industry. If the variance of output between firms σ_x^2 tends to increase with increases of var X, this decrease of industry's average profit is even larger than is indicated by expression 8.8.

Equation 8.7 permits us to compare profit under conditions of certainty with the average profit of the industry under uncertainty. Assume that under certainty demand and supply are always in equilibrium. Then, under certainty,

$$\beta_0 - \beta_1 X = \frac{2a}{k} X + b \qquad 8.9$$

and, the equilibrium level of output, $\tilde{X}$, is

$$\tilde{X} = \frac{\beta_0 - b}{\dfrac{2a}{k} + \beta_1}. \qquad 8.10$$

If industry's output under uncertainty is on average equal to $\tilde{X}$, then it follows from equation 8.7 that industry's average profit is less under these circumstances than under certainty.

Since var $X > 0$ and $\sigma_x{}^2 > 0$ under uncertainty, whereas both are zero under certainty, then, if $E(X) = \tilde{X}$ under uncertainty, average profit is less under uncertainty. If $E(X) = \tilde{X}$, industry's average profit is lower the greater var X and $E(\sigma_x{}^2)$.

Just taking account of convexity properties, it is possible to state a general theorem. Suppose that Π, which may depend quite generally on any finite number of moments of the distribution of x, output, between firms, is strictly concave in X. Suppose that $\partial^2\Pi/\partial X^2 < 0$, and let

$$\Pi = \Pi(X, \Gamma) \qquad\qquad 8.11$$

where $[\Gamma]$ is a vector of variables (moments) which influence Π. Then, if $\partial^2\Pi/\partial X^2 < 0$, if all X are not equal, and if $[\Gamma]$ is not random,

$$E[\Pi(X, \Gamma)] < \Pi(E[X], \Gamma). \qquad\qquad 8.12$$

Other things equal, "an increase in the variability" of X tends to decrease the average profit of the industry if the industry's profit function is strictly concave in X. The industry's profit function is bound to be strictly concave in X if the industry's revenue function is strictly concave in X and if the industry's total cost function is strictly convex in X.

But I should not like to give the impression that under no circumstance can price uncertainty raise industry profit. If at any point of time uncertainty leads to a monopoly-like restriction of output, it can raise the industry's profit above its level under certainty. Taking the quadratic example which is mentioned above, let $\tau(X)$ represent the industry's profit for any period if $\sigma_x{}^2 = 0$. Then, under certainty, industry's profit in every period is

$$\tau(\tilde{X}) = P(\tilde{X})\tilde{X} - \left\{\frac{a}{k}\tilde{X}^2 + b\tilde{X} + kc\right\} \qquad\qquad 8.13$$

and under uncertainty and for any particular period,

$$\Psi = \tau(X) - ka\sigma_x{}^2. \qquad\qquad 8.14$$

PRICE UNCERTAINTY AND INDUSTRY PROFIT

The maximum of $\tau(X)$ occurs for some output value X_0, which is less than $\tilde{X}$,[4] and, since $\tau(X)$ is a strictly concave function,[5]

$$\tau(X_0) > \tau(\tilde{X}).$$

If σ_x^2 is sufficiently small,

$$\tau(X_0) - ka\sigma_x^2 > \tau(\tilde{X})$$

and there are X-values in the neighborhood of X_0 such that

$$\tau(X) - ka\sigma_x^2 > \tau(\tilde{X}).$$

Hence, industry's profit can be higher under uncertainty than under certainty. If this is to occur, X must be less than $\tilde{X}$, but this is not sufficient. Even if $X = X_0$, industry's profit can be less than under certainty if σ_x^2 is large. Consider average profit over time. If price uncertainty is going to raise average profit above its certainty level, it is necessary for $E(X)$ to be less than $\tilde{X}$. But, as even a cursory examination of equation 8.7 indicates, this is far from sufficient. It is evident from this equation that even if $E(X) = X_0$, average profit under uncertainty can be lower than under certainty provided that var X and $E(\sigma_x^2)$ are sufficiently large.

For some purposes, it is more informative to cast the analysis in terms of shadow ("predicted") prices rather than in terms of output. This can easily be done for the above quadratic case. Where x_i represents the output of the ith firm in any period, let $\hat{p}_i$ represent the value of p such that

$$x_i = \frac{p_i - b}{2a}. \qquad 8.15$$

[4] If industry's profit is to be at a maximum the marginal costs of all firms must be equal and in turn equal to the industry's marginal revenue. Let the industry's supply curve, constructed on the assumption that the marginal costs of all firms are equal, be represented by $S(X)$. Let $P(X)$ represent the industry's demand curve, and suppose that $P(X) = S(X)$ for a unique output level $\tilde{X}$. Now, if $P(X)$ is a monotonically decreasing function of X, $R'(X)$, marginal revenue, is less than average revenue for $X > 0$. Consequently, if $S(X)$ is a monotonically increasing function of X and does not increase at an infinite rate, $S(X) = R'(X)$ for a value X_0 which is less than $\tilde{X}$. X_0 maximizes industry's profit and is less than $\tilde{X}$.

[5] $\dfrac{d^2\tau}{dX^2} = -2\beta_1 - \dfrac{2a}{k} < 0.$

Since $\hat{p}_i$ represents the ith firm's shadow price for any particular period, industry's profit can be expressed in terms of actual price and shadow prices by substituting

$$x_i = \frac{\hat{p}_i - b}{2a} \qquad (i = 1, \ldots, k) \qquad 8.16$$

into expression 8.3.

Represent the average shadow price in the industry at any time point as

$$\mu_{\hat{p}} = \frac{1}{k} \sum_{i=1}^{k} \hat{p}_i$$

and let

$$\sigma_{\hat{p}}^2 = \frac{1}{k} \sum_{i=1}^{k} (\mu_{\hat{p}} - \hat{p}_i)^2.$$

The variance of shadow prices between firms is represented by $\sigma_{\hat{p}}^2$. Since

$$X = k \left(\frac{\mu_{\hat{p}} - b}{2a} \right), \qquad 8.17$$

and using 8.16,

$$\Pi = \beta_0 X - \beta_1 X^2 - k \left\{ \frac{1}{k} \sum_{i=1}^{k} \left[a \left(\frac{\hat{p}_i - b}{2a} \right)^2 + b \frac{\hat{p}_i - b}{2a} + c \right] \right\}$$

$$= \beta_0 k \left\{ \frac{\mu_{\hat{p}} - b}{2a} \right\} - \beta_1 k^2 \left\{ \frac{\mu_{\hat{p}} - b}{2a} \right\}^2$$

$$- k \left\{ \frac{\mu_{\hat{p}}^2 + \sigma_{\hat{p}}^2 - 2\mu_{\hat{p}}b + b^2}{4a} + \frac{b\mu_{\hat{p}} - b^2}{2a} + c \right\}.$$

$$8.18$$

From this equation,

$$\frac{\partial \Pi}{\partial \sigma_{\hat{p}}^2} = -\frac{k}{4a} < 0. \qquad 8.19$$

From equation 8.18, if other things are constant, an increase in the variance of shadow prices reduces the industry's total profit. This is at odds with Knight's dictum that if entrepreneurs "estimate correctly on the whole" then their aggregate profit is unaffected. For example, take the case in which industry's output is $\tilde{X}$ under certainty. Then, under certainty, industry's profit is $\tau(\tilde{X})$. If, under uncertainty, $\mu_{\hat{p}} = P(\tilde{X})$, industry's profit will be

$$\Pi = \tau(\tilde{X}) - \frac{k}{4a} \sigma_{\hat{p}}^2,$$

which, if $\sigma_{\hat{p}}^2 > 0$, is less than under certainty. Hence some modification of Knight's view is required.

If entrepreneurs as a group overestimate their prospects, they are bound, as a group, to earn less than under certainty. If $\mu_{\hat{p}} > P(\tilde{X})$, then $X > \tilde{X}$, and not only is the industry's profit less than under certainty but so also is the profit of each firm. However, if entrepreneurs as a group underestimate their prospects, industry's profit may be but is not necessarily, higher than under certainty. Although in this case the profits of all firms may be higher than under certainty, circumstances can arise in which the profits of some and even all are less than under certainty. The last two possibilities may occur even if $\mu_{\hat{p}} = P(X_0)$.

It is now possible to express average or expected profit in terms of the moments of shadow prices. Taking the expectation or average value of equation 8.18,

$$E[\Pi] = \beta_0 k \left\{ \frac{E(\mu_{\hat{p}}) - b}{2a} \right\} -$$

$$- \beta_1 k^2 \left\{ \frac{E(\mu_{\hat{p}})^2 + \text{var } \mu_{\hat{p}} - 2bE(\mu_{\hat{p}}) + b^2}{4a^2} \right\}$$

$$- k \left\{ \frac{E(\mu_{\hat{p}}) + \text{var } \mu_{\hat{p}} + E(\sigma_{\hat{p}}^2) - 2E(\mu_{\hat{p}})b + b^2}{4a} \right.$$

$$\left. + \frac{bE(\mu_{\hat{p}}) - b^2 + c}{2a} \right\}. \qquad 8.20$$

From equation 8.20,

$$\frac{\partial E[\Pi]}{\partial \text{ var } \mu_{\hat{p}}} = - \frac{\beta_1 k^2}{4a^2} - \frac{k}{4a} < 0 \qquad 8.21$$

and

$$\frac{\partial E[\Pi]}{\partial E[\sigma_{\hat{p}}^2]} = - \frac{k}{4a} < 0. \qquad 8.22$$

It follows from equation 8.20 that, if other things remain unchanged, an increase in the variance of $\mu_{\hat{p}}$, the industry's average shadow price, reduces the industry's expected profit. Other things remaining equal, an increase in $E[\sigma_{\hat{p}}^2]$ also decreases the industry's expected profit. If as var $\mu_{\hat{p}}$ increases $E[\sigma_{\hat{p}}^2]$ increases, then the decline of expected profit as a result of an increase in var $\mu_{\hat{p}}$ is even greater than is suggested by equation 8.21.

Let us compare the industry's expected profit under certainty with that under uncertainty. It follows from equation 8.20 that if, under uncertainty, $E(\mu_{\hat{p}}) = P(\tilde{X})$ and if [var $\mu_{\hat{p}}$, $E(\sigma_{\hat{p}}^2)$] > [0, 0], then the industry's average profit is less under uncertainty than under certainty. If the industry's average shadow price is on average equal to the price under certainty, expected profit of the industry under conditions of uncertainty is less than under certainty. If $E(\mu_{\hat{p}}) > P(\tilde{X})$, average profit of the industry is certainly less than under certainty, but we cannot assert that the average profit of *every* firm is less than under certainty. If industry's average profit is to be raised by price uncertainty, the average shadow price must on average be less than $P(\tilde{X})$. When compared with actual prices, shadow prices must on average be biased downward. This is a necessary but not a sufficient condition for price uncertainty to increase the expected profit of the industry. Even if $E(\mu_{\hat{p}})$ = $P(X_0)$, industry's average profit can be less than under certainty,[6] and it is even possible for the average profit of every firm to be less than under certainty.

Although we cannot, on theoretical grounds, exclude the possibility of price uncertainty "causing" a rise in industry's average profit, our results indicate that this is only a possible outcome under unusual conditions. For such an outcome, the average shadow price must be biased downward and the variances of $\mu_{\hat{p}}$ and $\hat{p}$ must be sufficiently small. If any statement is warranted on *a priori* grounds, it would seem that price uncertainty is almost certain to reduce an industry's average profit below its level under certainty.

[6] This will be the case if var $\mu_{\hat{p}}$ and $E(\sigma_{\hat{p}}^2)$ are large enough.

Again, consider a slight generalization. Assume that the industry's average profit for any sub-period is a function of $\mu_{\hat{p}}$ and a vector of other moments of $\hat{p}$, $[\eta]$. Industry's profit for any sub-period can be represented as

$$\Pi = \Pi(\mu_{\hat{p}}, \eta). \qquad 8.23$$

Now, if $\partial^2 \Pi / \partial \mu_{\hat{p}}^2 < 0$, if all $\mu_{\hat{p}}$ values are not equal, and if $[\eta]$ is not random,

$$E[\Pi(\mu_{\hat{p}}, \eta)] < \Pi(E[\mu_{\hat{p}}], \eta). \qquad 8.24$$

If all values of $\mu_{\hat{p}}$ are equal, the two expressions in 8.24 are equal. If industry's profit is a strictly concave function in $\mu_{\hat{p}}$, if $E[\mu_{\hat{p}}]$ is constant and other things also, variability in $\mu_{\hat{p}}$ reduces the industry's average profit. Take the case in which $E[\mu_{\hat{p}}] = P(\tilde{X})$. Then, given the conditions preceding equation 8.24,

$$E[\Pi(\mu_{\hat{p}}, \eta)] < \Pi(P[\tilde{X}], \eta), \qquad 8.25$$

and if, under certainty, $[\eta] = [\eta^\circ]$, and if

$$\Pi(P[\tilde{X}], \eta^\circ) \geq \Pi(P[\tilde{X}], \eta), \qquad 8.26$$

average profit under uncertainty is less than under certainty. This is so if we can assume that the industry's average shadow price under uncertainty is on average equal to the product's price under certainty.

Our results indicate that price uncertainty leads to an increase in an industry's average profit only under exceptional circumstances. If costs differ between firms but marginal costs are increasing, this conclusion is unlikely to be significantly affected. Also, if the demand and supply curves are subject to shifts, e.g., by variation in their "constant" term, the analysis can be readily extended to take account of this. Furthermore, we need not assume linear demand and supply functions, but can obtain, as is already indicated, broad results by considering the convexity qualities of the demand and supply functions.

C. Price Variability and the
Industry's Average Profit

In the particular quadratic case considered above, it is evident that increased price instability must always be associated with a reduction in industry's average profit if the average market price remains constant. This is so, because if

$$P = \beta_0 - \beta_1 X, \qquad 8.27$$

$$E(P) = \beta_0 - \beta_1 E[X] \qquad 8.28$$

and

$$\operatorname{var} P = \beta_1^2 \operatorname{var} X. \qquad 8.29$$

If $E[X]$ is constant so is $E(P)$, and var P increases with var X. Hence it follows from equation 8.7 that an increase in the variance of market price must, if $E(P)$ is constant, be associated with a decline in the industry's average profit.[7] The increased price variability, in this case, arises due to increased error. If both the demand and the supply curves are stationary, a decline in industry's average profit tends to be associated with increased price instability if the industry profit function is strictly concave in X.

If we take the case in which *certainty exists*, and the demand curve is subject to variation over time but not the firm's costs, then increased price instability tends to increase industry's average profit if marginal costs are increasing. Take the case in which all marginal cost curves are identical and linear. Then,

[7] From equation 8.28,

$$E[X] = \frac{E(P - \beta_0)}{\beta_1}$$

and from equation 8.29,

$$\operatorname{var} X = \frac{1}{\beta_1^2} \operatorname{var} P.$$

Substituting these values into equation 8.7 and supposing $E[ka\sigma_x^2]$ to be constant,

$$\frac{\partial E(\pi)}{\partial \operatorname{var} P} = -\frac{1}{\beta_1} - \frac{a}{k\beta_1^2} < 0.$$

If $E[ka\sigma_x^2]$ tends to increase with var P, the decrease of $E(\pi)$ for an increase of var P is even greater than indicated above.

if $E[P(\tilde{X})]$ is constant, industry's average profit increases as var $P(\tilde{X})$ increases. This follows immediately from an extension of our theorems for individual firms, since the industry's profit is the summation of individual profits (see Chapter V).

However, if certainty exists, but the variation in market price occurs due to a variation in costs, the demand function remaining stationary, we can no longer be certain that an increase in the variability of $P(\tilde{X})$ will increase the average profit of the industry if marginal cost is increasing with increases of output. Even in the quadratic case, if the linear marginal costs are subject to shifting and the demand function is stationary, industry's average profit *can* decline as var $P(\tilde{X})$ increases, $E[P(\tilde{X})]$ remaining constant. To convince oneself of this, it is enough to consider the limiting case in which the marginal cost of the industry's output is a constant function of output. If marginal cost is subject to variation over time, if $E[P(\tilde{X})]$ is constant, and if average fixed cost is constant, then the industry's total average cost is constant, but, given that the industry's demand curve is linear and downward sloping, the industry's average total revenue declines with increases in the variance of $P(\tilde{X})$. In fact, under these conditions, increased price variability, Δ var $P(\tilde{X})$, *decreases* the industry's average aggregate profit by $(1/\beta_1)\Delta$ var $P(\tilde{X})$.

D. Conclusion

Clearly, the analysis of this subject can be carried further along lines similar to those indicated by Nelson's work[8] without making assumptions as special as his. The virtue of our analysis so far has been its comparative generality. It has indicated that while price uncertainty can increase the average profit of an industry, such an increase is exceptional. Other things equal, increased price uncertainty tends, under very general conditions, to decrease the average profit of an industry.

[8] R. R. Nelson, "Uncertainty, Prediction and Competitive Equilibrium," *The Quarterly Journal of Economics*, vol. 75 (1961), pp. 41–62. The question of entry has not been discussed above. It would, however, be too naive to suggest that it depends only on the average profit earned in the industry.

Other things equal, an increase in the variability of the price of the product can either decrease or increase an industry's average profit depending upon the circumstances. If certainty exists and the increased variability arises from a variation of the demand function, then, under very general conditions, increased price instability is associated with increased average profit for the industry. But under other conditions, some of which are suggested above, increased price instability is associated with a decline in the industry's average profit.

CHAPTER IX

Errors, Aggregate Output, and Forward Prices

A. Introduction

In this chapter, the effect of price uncertainty upon the economy's level of aggregate production is of central interest. The discussion of this matter suggests that, under quite general conditions, price uncertainty reduces the aggregate production of the economy to a level below its production frontier. If this is so, we are naturally prompted to ask the question of whether there exist any policies which can reduce uncertainty and increase the aggregate production and consumption of the economy. Forward price schemes are considered as a means for achieving this result, and it is concluded that they can, under certain circumstances, increase the aggregate output and consumption of the economy.

Once more, comparatively simple formulations are used in the analysis. The static decision-making assumptions, which have eliminated much complication in previous analysis, are also used here. First, formulations are introduced which assume a fixed allocation of factors to each of the firms in the economy, and then a model is introduced which permits the unimpeded transfer of factors between firms but assumes a fixed allocation of factors to each type of product. The discussion is then extended to the case in which factors can move freely throughout the economy.

B. Formulation based on a Fixed Allocation of Resources to Each Firm

In this formulation, it is supposed that each firm has a given allocation of resources. To consider the proposition that price uncertainty decreases the aggregate production of the economy, we first consider a two-product case and later generalize it to more products and to a larger set of circumstances. Let us make the following assumptions for the two-product case:

(i) The economy produces only two products, X_1 and X_2.

(ii) Each of the $i = 1, \ldots, k$ firms in the economy must "decide" on its output of these commodities n periods in advance of actual output (equals sales), $n \geq 1$. The only interdependence of production in time is that the "planned" output of $t - n$ equals the actual output of t.

(iii) Available to each firm is a fixed quantity of factors of production at a fixed cost.

(iv) The output possibilities of each firm are independent of those elsewhere in the economy. Thus external economies and diseconomies of production are ruled out.

(v) Each firm's output falls on its production possibility frontier. For the ith firm this frontier can be represented by a strictly concave function $x_{2i} = f_i(x_{1i}), i = 1, \ldots, k$, where x_{2i} represents the output of X_2 by the ith firm and x_{1i} represents its output of X_1.

(vi) Each firm's production possibilities form a convex compact set.

Take the simplest case in which all firms have the same production possibility frontiers. It follows from the strict concavity of the production transformation frontiers that unless firms produce the same production combination, the production of the economy will be below its maximum; i.e., it will be possible to increase the output of at least one product without decreasing that of any other. If as a result of uncertainty, all x_{1i} are not equal, the economy's output will not be at a maximum. Taking any instance in which all the x_{1i} are not equal and representing the economy's aggregate output of X_1 by X°_1, then it is easily shown that the economy's output would be greater if each firm had produced X°_1/k. The output of X_2 would be increased while that of X_1 remains unchanged. Other equalized combinations, besides $[f(X^\circ_1/k), X^\circ_1/k]$ will also increase aggregate output.

Now, turning to supply functions, let $\hat{p}_{1i}$ represent the ith firm's shadow price for product X_1 in some period t, and let $\hat{p}_{2i}$ represent that for product X_2. Then, given the above conditions, the supply functions of the ith firm can be expressed as a function of $\hat{p}_{1i}/\hat{p}_{2i}$. Letting ν_i represent $\hat{p}_{1i}/\hat{p}_{2i}$, the supply functions of each firm can be represented as

$$x_{1i} = \xi_i(\nu_i) \qquad i = 1, \ldots, k, \qquad\qquad 9.1$$

and

$$x_{2i} = \Phi_i(\nu_i) \qquad i = 1, \ldots, k. \qquad\qquad 9.2$$

These functions are concave but not necessarily strictly concave functions of ν_i. If all the functions $\{\xi_i(\nu_i); i = 1, \ldots, k\}$ are the same, then so too are those in expression 9.2, and it is readily shown that if all ν_i are not the same, and if no firm produces a corner-point combination of output, that equalizing the shadow price ratios of all firms to $\nu^* = \dfrac{1}{k} \sum\limits_{i=1}^{k} \nu_i$ will increase aggregate output. It will increase the economy's aggregate output of both X_1 and X_2, and there will be a number of other equalized rates in the neighborhood of ν^* which will also increase aggregate output. By ruling out corner-point output solutions, we limit the relevant portions of the supply curves to *strictly* concave ones. If corner-point output combinations are allowed, then equalizing price ratios to ν^* will either increase aggregate output or leave it unchanged.

Suppose that each firm's production frontier function is differentiable and that no firm produces a production bundle at a corner-point in its set of production possibilities. Then, given the above conditions, the output of the economy will not be at a maximum unless the rates of transformation of the products are the same for all firms. The firms' shadow price ratios must all be equal, otherwise the aggregate output of the economy will be below its maximum value.

Under these conditions, the economy's production frontier can be represented by a strictly concave differentiable function. Suppose that it can be stated explicitly as

$$X_2 = H(X_1). \qquad\qquad 9.3$$

If shadow price ratios or rates of technical transformation are not the same for all firms, output falls below the economy's frontier and is, say, $[X^\circ_1, X^\circ_2]$. Consequently, equalized rates of product transformation,

$$\frac{dH}{dX_2} = H'(X_1) \qquad\qquad 9.4$$

anywhere in the range $X^\circ_1 \leq X_1 \leq H^{-1}(X^\circ_2)$ will, if $H(X_1)$ decreases monotonically, increase aggregate output. The strict concavity of $H(X_1)$ ensures that there are a number of equalized rates of product transformation which increase aggregate output.

Given the above conditions, if the shadow price ratios of all firms are not the same, their rates of product transformation are not all the same and there is a range of equalized shadow price ratios, or rates of product transformation, which increase the aggregate output of the economy. Under certain conditions, forward price schemes can equalize the shadow price ratios and bring about an increase in aggregate production, and this will be discussed below.

These results can be generalized to cover more than the two-product case. Suppose that the economy can produce q products and represent the product transformation frontier of the ith firm by

$$\phi_i(x_1, x_2, \ldots, x_q) = 0, \qquad i = 1, \ldots, k. \qquad 9.5$$

It production is always on this frontier, is always in points which are strictly convex for the firm's convex set of production possibilities, and the function representing the frontier is differentiable, output will not be at a maximum for the economy unless the shadow price ratios of all firms are equal. Unless the rates of product transformation are equal for all firms, it will be possible to increase the output of at least one product without decreasing the output of any other. If the rates of product transformation are not equal for all firms, there are some equalized rates which will increase the aggregate output of the economy. These rates can sometimes be equalized by forward price schemes which, if the forward prices are suitably selected, can increase aggregate output. Let us consider this matter in more detail.

C. A Forward Price Scheme

In order to see that a range of forward price policies[1] may increase the aggregate output and consumption of the economy, let us consider a particular forward price scheme. Imagine a forward price scheme which satisfies the following conditions:

(i) The State (which may operate through its agents) is the sole purchaser of the output of firms and the sole reseller to consumers.

(ii) The price which the State is willing to pay for the output of all the products is set sufficiently far in advance for firms to adjust to them; e.g., given the above production model, the forward price for the output of t is known in $t - n$ or earlier.

(iii) The State fixes the price for sales to consumers. This is not an essential assumption.

(iv) Each firm aims to maximize its profit.

(v) Consumers spend all of their income, which equals the total income of producers. Again, this is not an essential assumption; investment can be allowed.

(vi) The administration of the forward price scheme requires an almost negligible proportion of resources, and this usage can be ignored.

Assume that the economy produces two products, that each firm always produces on its production frontier, which forms a differentiable function, that its production possibilities form a convex set and its output is always in a strictly convex point of the set, and that all the other production assumptions at the beginning of section A hold *mutatis mutandis*. Suppose that the

---

[1] For a definition of forward prices, see D. G. Johnson, *Forward Prices for Agriculture*, The University of Chicago Press, Chicago, 1947, pp. 10–12.

economy's production frontier can be represented by a strictly concave and differentiable function

$$X_2 = H(X_1).$$

Taking some sub-period t, let p_1 and p_2 represent the prices payable by consumers for products X_1 and X_2, and let p^*_1 and p^*_2 represent the forward prices which are payable to firms for their output of these products in period t. Letting Y represent the aggregate money income of period t, suppose that the respective aggregate demand for commodities X_1 and X_2 in that period can be represented by the respective functions

$$D_1 = D_1(Y, p_1, p_2) \qquad 9.6$$

and

$$D_2 = D_2(Y, p_1, p_2). \qquad 9.7$$

Thus the distribution of income is assumed to be an unimportant factor in the determination of the aggregate demand for the products. If S_1 and S_2 indicate the respective supplies of product X_1 and X_2 in period t,

$$Y = p^*_1 S_1 + p^*_2 S_2. \qquad 9.8$$

Furthermore, given the above assumptions, the supply of the products is a function of their relative forward prices. Where

$$\eta = \frac{p^*_1}{p^*_2},$$

the supply of X_1 and X_2 can be expressed respectively as

$$S_1 = S_1(\eta) \qquad 9.9$$

and

$$S_2 = S_2(\eta). \qquad 9.10$$

Suppose that as a result of price uncertainty shadow price ratios of firms are not all the same and that, consequently, aggregate output falls below the economy's frontier and stands at some level $[X^\circ_1, X^\circ_2]$ which, given that free competition exists, is also the economy's level of aggregate consumption.

Now, if the above forward price scheme had been in operation, could it have increased consumption? If the State operates the above forward price scheme, is there a range of $[p^*{}_1, p^*{}_2, p_1, p_2]$ values which will ensure that demands are less than or equal to available supplies and that the quantity consumed is greater than $[X^\circ{}_1, X^\circ{}_2]$? In other words, is there a range of $[p^*{}_1, p^*{}_2, p_1, p_2]$ values which ensures that the following conditions hold?

$$\left.\begin{array}{l} [D_1, D_2] \leq [S_1(\eta), S_2(\eta)] \\ [D_1, D_2] > [X^\circ{}_1, X^\circ{}_2] \end{array}\right\} \qquad 9.11$$

It is easily shown that a range of $[p^*{}_1, p^*{}_2, p_1, p_2]$ values satisfy conditions 9.11. Clearly, these conditions cannot be satisfied unless

$$[S_1(\eta), S_2(\eta)] > [X^\circ{}_1, X^\circ{}_2]. \qquad 9.12$$

Condition 9.12 is satisfied if the forward prices are set so that η falls anywhere in the range

$$\eta = \frac{\mathrm{d}H}{\mathrm{d}X_2} = H'(X_1), \qquad X^\circ{}_1 \leq X_1 \leq H^{-1}(X^\circ{}_2). \qquad 9.13$$

The argument surrounding equation 9.4 shows that a range of η-values increases aggregate output and, therefore, *a fortiori*, a range of $[p^*{}_1, p^*{}_2]$ values increases it. Let $\bar{\eta}$ represent any value which ensures that condition 9.12 is met, and suppose that not only is η determined but also $p^*{}_1$ and $p^*{}_2$ so that the value of Y is determined. Given this, then, if there is for every $[X_1, X_2]$ combination in the range $[X^\circ{}_1, X^\circ{}_2] < [X_1, X_2] \leq [S_1(\bar{\eta}), S_2(\bar{\eta})]$ a *unique* $[p_1, p_2]$ combination which results in its being demanded, there are a large number of $[p_1, p_2]$ values which ensure that conditions 9.11 are met.[2] Hence, a large number of $[p^*{}_1, p^*{}_2, p_1, p_2]$ values will guarantee

[2] Not only is Y determined once $p^*{}_1$ and $p^*{}_2$ are determined but so also is the distribution of money income.

For a detailed discussion of the relationship of aggregate demand to income and prices, see I. F. Pearce, *A Contribution to Demand Analysis*, Clarendon Press, Oxford, 1964, Ch. 3.

that conditions 9.11 are satisfied. Even under more general conditions, a range of forward prices may raise aggregate output and consumption to levels above that of free competition.

For some sets of price values which imply that conditions 9.11 are satisfied, the State, in operating the above forward price scheme, will finish the sub-period with uncleared surpluses of one or more of the products. This demonstrates that, if surpluses happen to arise during the operation of a forward price scheme, it is not thereby shown that the economy's consumption is lower than under free competition. If a forward price operates, if conditions 9.11 are satisfied, and if surpluses arise, these surpluses may be destroyed or be donated to separate economies, and the domestic economy's consumption will still be greater than under free competition.

Stocks have been excluded from the above analysis, but their introduction does not alter the general conclusion. However, it might be noted that even in cases where private firms would hold no stocks under free competition, a State which is operating a forward price scheme may find it worthwhile to carry stocks in order to allow sufficient margin for errors in its prices. Even though it may be costly to carry stock, the aggregate consumption of the community may as a result of the operation of the forward price scheme be greater than under free competition.

If a forward price scheme operates, there may be a large range of prices which raise the aggregate income and consumption of the community to levels above those under free competition. Even if surpluses should arise from the operation of these forward price schemes, aggregate consumption may be higher than in their absence. Of course, even if forward price schemes do happen to increase aggregate production and consumption, it does not necessarily follow that it is desirable to adopt them or that they increase "the welfare of society." Forward price schemes do not leave other things unaltered. They tend, for instance, to increase the authority of the State. While the above analysis can easily be extended to cover any finite number of products, its conclusion holds under a set of conditions which are wider than the above set. It is of interest to consider other conditions which imply that the conclusion holds.

D. A Formulation which Allows Some Mobility of Factors

Since forward price schemes, in practice, rarely if ever cover all products or commodities, let us show that these partial schemes can raise the aggregate output and consumption of the economy to levels above those under free competition and, further, that a range of forward prices may achieve this result. To demonstrate this for a model which permits mobility of factors among firms but not among products, assume the following conditions:

(i) There are $i = 1, \ldots, k$ firms in the economy which can produce $r = 1, \ldots, q$ different products.

(ii) The output of each product requires the input of only one variable factor. This assumption simplifies the analysis but is not essential to it.

(iii) Where L_r represents the variable factor which is specific to the rth product, its total supply L_r is inelastically supplied. This assumption can be relaxed.

(iv) The output of the rth product by the ith firm, x_{ri}, is a concave function of its input of the factor L_r. Where l_{ri} represents its input of factor L_r, the ith firm's output of the rth product is

$$x_{ri} = g_{ri}(l_{ri}), \qquad (r = 1, \ldots, q; i = 1, \ldots, k) \qquad 9.14$$

and

$$\frac{\mathrm{d}^2 x_{ri}}{\mathrm{d} l_{ri}^2} < 0. \qquad\qquad 9.15$$

Condition 9.15 implies diminishing marginal productivity.

(v) Each firm must decide upon its output and the input combination which is required to produce it n periods in advance of actual output, $n \geq 1$. The employment and allocation of inputs between firms is settled n periods in advance of output (equals sales) and is unalterable. Other than for this dependence in time, each output and input decision is independent in time.

(vi) No individual firm influences the price at which it buys a factor or the price at which it sells a product.

Consider the conditions which must be satisfied if the aggregate production of the economy is to be at a maximum. If no boundary solutions happen to be optimal, the following first-order conditions, where λ_r represents a Lagrange multiplier, must be satisfied:

$$\left. \begin{aligned} \frac{\mathrm{d}g_{rt}}{\mathrm{d}l_{rt}} &= \lambda_r \qquad (i = 1, \ldots, k; r = 1, \ldots, q) \\ \sum_{i=1}^{k} l_{rt} &= L_r \qquad (r = 1, \ldots, q) \end{aligned} \right\} \qquad 9.16$$

If aggregate production is to be at a maximum, then for each product the marginal productivity of the variable input which is specific to the product must be the same for all firms and the total available quantity of this input must be employed. If boundary solutions are ruled out, then the output of any product will not be at a maximum if the marginal productivity of the factor which is specific to it differs among firms. If marginal productivities of the factor differ among firms, it will be possible to increase the output of its product without increasing its aggregate employment.

If price uncertainty arises, the marginal physical productivity of a factor is, at any point of time, liable to differ for some firms. The price uncertainty which arises under free competition may, through differences of anticipations and behavior reactions, cause shadow prices to differ for firms which are supplying the same market. Suppose that the relevant price of factor L_r is known in period $t - n$ and represent it by w_r. Let $\hat{p}_{rt}$ denote the ith firm's shadow price for the rth product.

Then, in order to produce the rth product, the ith firm employs the factor L_r up to the point where the factor's shadow marginal revenue product equals its price; i.e., it employs the factor up to the point where

$$w_r = \frac{dg_{ri}}{dl_{ri}} \hat{p}_{ri} \qquad\qquad 9.17$$

or

$$\frac{dg_{ri}}{dl_{ri}} = \frac{w_r}{\hat{p}_{ri}}. \qquad\qquad 9.18$$

If w_r has the same value for all firms but not $\hat{p}_r$, it follows from equation 9.18 that the marginal physical productivity of the factor L_r is not the same for all firms. Since the production functions are strictly concave and boundary solutions are ruled out, this circumstance of divergent shadow prices implies that the aggregate output of the rth product is below its maximum. The price of factor L_r will tend to be the same for all firms if factors are completely mobile in $t - n$, if contracts are entered into then, and if sellers of factors are well informed about price offers.

But even if the price of the factor L_r differs among firms or is not known by them all, so that a shadow price term of $\hat{w}_{ri}$ needs to be substituted for w_r in equation 9.18, price uncertainty may reduce the aggregate output of the product. If contracts for hiring the factor L_r, which is required for the output of t, are settled in $t - n$ and if the ratios $\hat{w}_{ri}/\hat{p}_{ri}$ are not equal for all firms which produce the rth product, then it is possible to increase the output of the product without increasing the total employment of the factor L_r, it being assumed that no corner-point solutions arise. Under these circumstances, there are a number of equalized shadow price ratios $\hat{w}_{ri}/\hat{p}_{ri}$ which increase the output of the rth product for the same or a smaller total employment of the factor L_r. If when the rth product's shadow price ratios equalize at these values, the shadow price ratios for other products remain unchanged, the aggregate output of the economy increases.

In order to bring out the importance of the convexity assumptions in this analysis, let us suppose that all firms have the same production function for the rth product. The production function of the ith firm for the rth product can be represented as

$$x_{ri} = g_r(l_{ri}). \qquad 9.19$$

If function 9.19 is strictly concave (and is not necessarily differentiable) then, for any given aggregate employment of L_r, the aggregate output of the rth product will not be at a maximum unless all firms employ an equal quantity of the factor L_r. If all values of l_{ri}, $i = 1, \ldots, k$, are *not* equal, it follows from the properties of *strictly* concave functions that[3]

$$\sum_{i=1}^{k} \frac{1}{k} g_r(l_{ri}) < g_r \left(\frac{1}{k} \sum_{i=1}^{k} l_{ri} \right) \qquad 9.20$$

and, hence, that

$$k \sum_{i=1}^{k} \frac{1}{k} g_r(l_{ri}) < k g_r \left(\frac{1}{k} \sum_{i=1}^{k} l_{ri} \right). \qquad 9.21$$

Given strict concavity, the expressions on both sides of proposition 9.20 can only be equal if all l_{ri} are equal. Expression 9.21 indicates that in this case the economy's aggregate output of the rth product is not a maximum unless all firms employ the same quantity of factor L_r. If all l_{ri}, $i = 1, \ldots, k$, are not equal, there are a number of equalized shadow price ratios, i.e., equalized values of $\hat{w}_{ri}/\hat{p}_{ri}$, which increase the output of the rth product for the same or a smaller total employment of the factor L_r.

If the production function is concave but not necessarily strictly so, only a weak inequality holds for the values on both sides of expression 9.21. In some such cases, a difference in the l_{ri} values may occur, and yet production of the rth product

---

[3] See G. H. Hardy, J. E. Littlewood, and G. Polya, *Inequalities*, Cambridge University Press, Cambridge, 1934, p. 74, or S. Karlin, *Matrix Games, Programming and Mathematical Economics*, Vol. I, Addison–Wesley Publishing Company, Reading, 1959, pp. 404–405.

is at a maximum for the aggregate amount of L_r which is employed. Of course, if g_r happens to be a strictly convex function, the inequality of expression 9.21 is reversed. If, in addition to its being strictly concave, the function g_r is differentiable, then if the shadow price ratios $\hat{w}_{rt}/\hat{p}_{rt}$ are not all the same and if no boundary solutions occur, the l_{rt} values are not all the same and the production of the rth product is below its maximum for the employed quantity of L_r.

To illustrate some of these points, let us take an example such as that depicted in Figure 9.1. For ease of exposition, assume that only two firms produce the rth product. Then, the total employment of the factor L_r is $L_r = l_{r1} + l_{r2}$ and its average employment per firm is $\mu_r = \frac{1}{2}l_{r1} + \frac{1}{2}l_{r2}$. The production function which is shown in Figure 9.1 is strictly concave, and the two firms are shown as employing the differing quantities $l°_{r1}$ and $l°_{r2}$ of the factor L_r. In this case, their average output of the rth product is $x°_r$ and the economy's total output of it is $2x°_r$. If both firms happen to employ μ_r of factor L_r, this leaves the factor's aggregate employment unchanged and increases the economy's aggregate output of the rth product to $2x_r^1$, and the output of x_r is at a maximum for the employed quantity of L_r. But it is also obvious that any equalized employment of L_r in the range $l_r^1 < l_r \leq \mu_r$ will increase the aggregate output of the rth product without increasing the employment of factor L_r. Since the set

$$\{(x_r, l_r): 0 \leq x_r \leq g_r(l_r), \, l°_{r1} \leq l_r \leq \mu_r\}$$

is compact and convex, and since it is strictly convex in all points on its boundary portion $g_r(l_r)$, there are a number of equalized shadow price ratios $\hat{w}_{rt}/\hat{p}_{rt}$ which imply equalized employment in the range $l_r^1 < l_r \leq \mu_r$ and, hence, increase the output of the rth product without increasing the employment of factor L_r. This is so because a compact convex set has at least one supporting hyperplane for each point in its boundary, and the collection of supporting hyperplanes for any two points which are in the boundary and strictly convex in the set differ. Since there is a range of points for $x_r = g(l_r)$,

$l^{\circ}{}_{r1} < l_r \leq \mu_r$, they have a range of corresponding but differing supporting hyperplanes.

If the function $g_r(l_r)$ is not only strictly concave but is also everywhere differentiable, then, if the shadow price ratios of all firms for the rth product are not the same and if no boundary solutions occur, the production of the rth product is below its maximum for the given employment of factor L_r. Strict

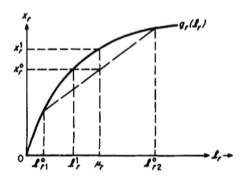

FIG. 9.1

concavity is not sufficient to ensure this result, since a function may be strictly concave and yet possess a number of corner-points. Taking the case illustrated, if $g_r(l_r)$ is differentiable, then there is for every $l_r > 0$ just one and only one tangent to each point on the function $g_r(l_r)$, and no two tangents have the same slope, since $g_r(l_r)$ is strictly concave. Consequently, every point on $g_r(l_r)$, $l_r > 0$, corresponds to a different shadow price ratio, and if the shadow price ratios of the two firms differ then so too does their employment of the factor L_r, and there exist a number of equalized shadow price ratios which will increase the aggregate output of the rth product without an increase in the employment of L_r.

Returning to the particular case above where the factor is

in inelastic supply for each product, it is not difficult to see that, if a forward price is set for any product, that aggregate output is increased, and the greater the number of products for which forward price schemes operate, the greater is aggregate output. Forward price schemes, by equalizing the shadow prices for any product—since the prices of the factor specific to it are assumed to equalize—do bring the marginal productivity of the factor for each firm into equality, and this must increase the output of the product, since the supply of $L_r(r = 1, \ldots, q)$ is assumed to be inelastic, $w_r(r = 1, \ldots, q)$ adjusting so that its total available quantity is employed. If, under the above conditions, shadow prices for the rth product are not all the same, then the State, by setting a forward price for this product at *any* level, will increase aggregate output. It is once more assumed that the cost of operating the forward price scheme is negligible and can be ignored. It will also be the case, unless demand is perfectly inelastic for the rth product, that the State may charge a price to the consumer within a range and yet consumption may be higher than in the absence of the forward price scheme, and here, again, surpluses of the rth product may arise and aggregate consumption can be higher than under free competition. In this case, the output of the economy is at a maximum when the State sets forward prices for all products. But even if the whole economy is not covered by forward price schemes, schemes covering only a limited range of products can increase aggregate consumption, and production and can do so for a *range* of forward prices.

Fortunately, this general result does not depend upon the assumption of inelasticity in the supply of factors. If the factors are specific to the products and not in inelastic supply, there may yet be a number of forward prices for each product which increase aggregate consumption and production. To convince oneself of this, it is only necessary to take the simple case in which the supply of each factor rises with its money price. If this is so, and if the money price of a factor rises with the price of the product to which it is specific, then, clearly, if shadow price ratios of the rth product differ under uncertainty there are a number of equalized forward prices which increase the output of the product without increasing the employment of the factor and so increase aggregate output. However, we can even go further than this and drop the assumption that factors are specific to any product.[4]

E. Further Generalization

The conditions which must be satisfied if production is to be at a maximum have been systematically explored in welfare economics. The general propositions which have been obtained in welfare economics enable us to extend the above results. If

- (i) each firm's set of production possibilities is compact and convex;
- (ii) if its production is always such that it cannot, given its employed resources, increase its output of any product without decreasing that of another; and
- (iii) if it always falls in a differentiable segment of the boundary of its set of production possibilities and at points which are strictly convex in this set;

then the economy's production is not at a maximum if shadow price ratios differ in such a way that rates of technical substitution of factors are not equal for all firms, that rates of product transformation are not equal, or that the marginal physical productivity of any factor is not the same everywhere.[5]

---

[4] For some examples which involve quadratic production functions and, therefore, only the variance and mean shadow price values of firms, see C. Tisdell, "Uncertainty and Pareto Optimality," *Economic Record*, vol. 39 (1963), pp. 405–412; C. Tisdell, "A Rejoinder," *Economic Record*, vol. 40 (1964), pp. 590–596. In an example of the rejoinder one factor is considered as being mobile throughout the whole economy, and it is shown that if a forward price is set for any product equal to the alternative average shadow price under free competition, or for some range of values less than this, that aggregate output increases.

[5] See, for example, J. M. Henderson and R. E. Quandt, *Microeconomic Theory*, McGraw–Hill Book Company, New York, 1958, p. 205. In the above discussion, external economies or diseconomies of production are ruled out.

In such circumstances, forward price schemes may increase aggregate consumption and production and do so for a range of price possibilities.

Other extensions of the argument are possible. It is not necessary to suppose that all firms produce every product or to assume that all production is subject to decreasing returns. If some industries are subject to increasing costs and others to decreasing costs, forward price schemes in an industry which has increasing costs may, if price uncertainty previously existed, raise aggregate output and the economy's consumption. But under an even wider range of circumstances than those indicated above, forward price schemes can raise aggregate production for a range of price possibilities. Even in some cases where the production possibility sets of firms are not convex, e.g., involve discontinuities or areas of increasing returns, forward price schemes may yet increase the economy's aggregate output.

F. Implications of the Preceding Results for Calculation in a Socialist Economy

The previous analysis has some implications for calculation in a socialist economy. A historic debate upon the question of the optimal direction of production in a socialist economy took place in the 1920's and 1930's, with notable contributions by such economists as Barone, von Mises, Hayek, Lange, and Taylor.[6] Hayek maintained that, although the socialist state could in principle organize production so that Pareto optimality is achieved, this is a sheer impossibility in practice. This must be especially the case if the socialist state tries to organize production directly, since a myriad of equations

[6] E. Barone, "The Ministry of Production in the Collectivist State," pp. 245–290 in Collectivist Economic Planning, F. A. von Hayek, ed., George Routledge and Sons, London, 1935. Also, in the same book, L. von Mises, "Economic Calculation in the Socialist Commonwealth," pp. 87–130. In On the Economic Theory of Socialism, B. Lippincott, ed., The University of Minnesota Press, Minneapolis, 1938: O. Lange "On the Economic Theory of Socialism," pp. 55–142; and F. M. Taylor, "The Guidance of Production in a Socialist State," pp. 41–54.

will need to be solved and the process of information gathering will be immense.

But neither Taylor nor Lange saw a socialist economy as solving its allocation and pricing problem in this way. Lange sees the Central Planning Board as setting prices for products, as directing "firms" which operate the State-owned resources to maximize profit upon the basis of these, consumers being left freedom of choice. He envisages the Planning Board as determining the price parameters in the following way: "The right prices are simply found out by watching the quantities demanded and the quantities supplied and by raising the price of a commodity or service whenever there is an excess of demand over supply and lowering it whenever the reverse is the case, until, by trial and error, the price is found at which demand and supply are in balance."[7] The process is similar to that in a free competitive market.

But Lange goes further. He claims possible allocative superiority of the socialist trial and error procedure when compared with the free competitive market. This claim is made on the grounds that "the Central Planning Board has a much wider knowledge of what is going on in the whole economic system than any private entrepreneur can ever have, and consequently, may be able to reach the right equilibrium prices by a *much shorter* series of successive trials than a competitive market actually does."[8]

The relevance of the preceding discussion will now be apparent. If the Planning Board lets producers know the prices of their products sufficiently far in advance of production, then even if the Board's prices are no closer to equilibrium than under free competition, or even further from it, production and consumption may be greater than under free competition since shadow prices will be brought into equality. In a large number of cases, if the Board sets the forward price equal to the average shadow price of the product under free competition. it raises the economy's aggregate output to a level above that under free competition. The Central Planning

<hr>

[7] O. Lange, *op. cit.*, p. 89.   [8] *Ibid.*

Board does not require a wider knowledge than the "average private entrepreneur" in order to raise the economy's aggregate output above the level under free competition.

Socialism is not required for the operation of the type of production system which Lange and Taylor envisage. Even if the means of production are privately owned, a board or boards may control production along Lange's lines by setting forward prices and operating associated schemes. Already, many agricultural marketing boards and similar authorities in "capitalist" countries operate along these or similar lines.

G. An Influence of Price Support Schemes and Price Stabilization Schemes on Production

As shown, forward price schemes can, under a wide range of circumstances, raise the economy's aggregate output and consumption above its level under free competition. They can do this by eliminating price uncertainty (at least in the short run) and equalizing firms' shadow prices for products.

However, aggregate production can also be increased if price uncertainty is reduced rather than eliminated. For example, if a situation such as that depicted in Figure 9.1 arises and the production functions for the rth product are quadratic, with the factor L_r in inelastic supply, any reduction in the variance of the shadow price of the product among firms will increase aggregate output. In cases where State marketing authorities stipulate a minimum price for a product, stipulate a maximum and a minimum price, or otherwise restrict the range of price possibilities by some "stabilization" scheme and give suitable guarantees in advance for these prices, the dispersion of shadow prices among firms may be reduced. This being so, there may exist a range of price policies, e.g., a range of support prices, which increase the economy's aggregate output. Again, surpluses may arise and aggregate consumption be higher than in the absence of the price support and stabilization schemes.

But one ought to be cautious in interpreting these assertions. It is not asserted that any price support scheme or stabilization scheme will increase aggregate consumption and production in the vector sense. But it is maintained that, if surpluses arise under such schemes, we cannot conclude *ipso facto* that the allocation of resources is inferior to that under free competition. It is also suggested that a *range* of price policies can, if such schemes operate, raise aggregate output above its level under free competition. To determine the extent of this range in any particular instance, we would, of course, need empirical evidence on the range of shadow prices (or "anticipated" prices) which are liable to occur under free competition.[9]

Very little has been said about the mechanics of operating different forward price schemes, but some important optimal control problems are involved. How far ahead should forward prices be fixed? Should the prices for periods further away be stipulated to fall within an increasing range, the price of the next period alone being certain? In considering the last question one needs to take account of the fact that the marketing authority is continually *learning*. On the one hand, it is desirable to have scope for variation in future prices so that the marketing authority can keep demand and supply in "some sort of balance," and, on the other, it is desirable to reduce the range of possibilities to some extent so that, taking account of the interdependencies of production in time, uncertainty is reduced and aggregate production is increased. We can easily imagine forward price schemes which increase aggregate production and yet do not commit the marketing authority to a rigid price policy over a long interval of time. Already our existing knowledge is such that we can specifically formalize and solve many of the problems which are involved in considering models which allow for learning. It seems that these control problems are important for both socialist and modified capitalist economies and deserve more than a superficial treatment.

[9] Soper and Webb, besides raising several other interesting points, suggest that the effect of the dispersion may be, in practice, of small magnitude. See, C. S. Soper and L. Webb, "Tisdell on Uncertainty and Pareto Optimality," *Economic Record*, vol. 40 (1964), pp. 581–590.

H. Conclusion

The theory has touched upon matters of considerable practical importance for socialist and capitalist economies.[10] It has shown that under a wide range of conditions price uncertainty reduces the economy's aggregate output given its employed resources. It is further shown that forward price schemes can, under a variety of circumstances, raise an economy's level of output and consumption above its level under free competition and may do so even if they create surpluses. Such an increase can occur even if the boards which operate the forward price schemes do not have predictive ability superior to that possessed by the "average" entrepreneur in a freely competitive market.

However, one should be careful in basing any normative propositions on the above positive statements, for forward price schemes also have several other effects. For instance, they increase the power of the State, and for most of us this will be an offsetting factor, though not necessarily an overriding one. Again, in their actual operation they may create such a distortion in the composition of production that they decrease the welfare of consumers. Such distortions may arise because of the political pressure of producers on the policies of the marketing boards. Furthermore, these schemes may alter the distribution of income, equalizing the profits of firms operating under identical cost conditions and eliminating any additional profit which previously arose for those with superior predictive ability. Yet the argument does indicate that the existence of surpluses or other evidence of an excess of supply over demand does not indicate, *ipso facto*, that if a forward price or quasi-forward price scheme is operating that consumers are worse off than under free competition.

---

[10] Within a short space, J. R. Hicks deals with several implications of risk and uncertainty for economic efficiency in capitalist and socialist economies. He not only touches on questions which are discussed above but on some important additional ones. See J. R. Hicks, *Value and Capital*, 2nd edn., The Clarendon Press, Oxford 1946 Ch. X, "Equilibrium and Disequilibrium."

CHAPTER X

On Dynamic Strands and Other Aspects
of the Analysis

A. Introduction

There seems to be little point in drawing hard and fast distinctions between "statics" and "dynamics" and in debating whether the previous models involve time in an essential way. It is somewhat more important to indicate some additional relationships and problems which arise "because of the existence of time." This chapter, besides indicating some of these relationships and problems, touches on such miscellaneous matters as technological uncertainty, equilibrium, and some of the possibilities for empirical research which are suggested by the analysis. It also concludes the discussion.

B. Additional Notes on Dynamics and the
Production Decisions of the Firm

Let us return to the production decisions of a purely competitive firm operating under price uncertainty and point out some of the problems which dynamics and, particularly, dynamic decision-making raise. In doing this, we shall find the contributions of Hicks, Hart, Tintner, and Theil to be relevant and, at a higher level of generality, von Neumann and Morgenstern's[1] conception of strategies.

---

[1] The following articles and work are particularly relevant for a further extension of the discussion: A. G. Hart, "Risk, Uncertainty, and the Unprofitability of Compounding Probabilities," pp. 110–118 in *Studies in Mathematical Economics and Econometrics*, O. Lange, F. McIntyre, and T. O. Yntema, eds., The University of Chicago Press, Chicago, 1942; J. R. Hicks, *Value and Capital*, 2nd edn., The Clarendon Press, Oxford, 1946, especially parts III and IV; H. Theil, *Economic Forecasts and Policy*, North–Holland Publishing Company, Amsterdam, 2nd revised edn., 1961, especially sections 8.2 and 8.6; G. Tintner, "A Contribution to the Nonstatic Theory of Production," pp. 92–109 in *Studies in Mathematical Economics and Econometrics*; J. von Neumann and O. Morgenstern, *Theory of Games and Economic Behavior*, Princeton University Press, Princeton, 1st edn., 1944, especially Ch. II.

On reviewing the general nature of the production models which have been discussed, we find that the major part of the analysis is based on static decision-making models, although a quadratic dynamic decision-making model was introduced. In these static decision-making models, although the decision of any period may determine the value of variables several periods later, it does not influence the *decisions* of any later period. In these models, variables whose values are influenced by a decision are not subject to further *controlled* variation after the decision is taken.

As an extreme static decision-making case, imagine that a firm has a fixed horizon and has to decide inflexibly upon its production combinations for a long time span which ends at the horizon. The combinations are to be inflexibly decided prior to the time span. For example, if time is treated as a discrete variable, a firm which is placed at t_0 might be imagined then to decide inflexibly on all of its production combinations for the periods $\{t_1, t_2, \ldots, t_N\}$. By assumption, it does not diverge from these values. However, this is not a realistic assumption if information changes during the time interval and there are no technical or institutional factors which prevent a divergence from point plans for production. Suppose that decisions have the quality that there is some last time point up to which they need not be made; they can be made at any time before that at no extra cost but cannot be varied after that date. Then, taking the example above, the alternative may arise of deciding inflexibly on production at t_0 for the whole interval $\{t_1, t_2, \ldots, t_N\}$ or delaying some production decisions. But if the information at the last time point for the delayed decisions is certain not to be different from that at t_0, then all production combinations can be inflexibly decided at t_0 for the whole interval without any "loss" to the firm.[2] The possible influence of calculation costs upon the optimal strategy are ignored.

[2] Naturally, if there is some probability that information will change by the time that the last possible time point for a decision is reached, then, in this model, there can be no loss from delaying it until that point, and there may be a gain by doing so.

The results of Chapters III and IV apply to the above extreme static decision-making cases, *mutatis mutandis*. Operating along lines similar to those adopted by Hicks in *Value and Capital*,[3] it is only necessary to place time subscripts upon the quantity values for the commodities and take into account the discount factor. The extension is straightforward.

But the static decision-making models of this analysis do not rule out possible changes of information over time or the possibility of adjusting to them. Imagine that decisions are placed in a sequence according to the last time point at which each can be made, and suppose that each can be delayed until this time point at no extra cost. The production decisions of the analysis are of this type, and it is supposed that any variable which is influenced by a decision is determined inflexibly and every decision is independent of every other. Consequently, each decision is "best" reached when its turn in the sequence arrives and the greatest possible amount of information, which is pertinent to it, is available.

But not all decisions are of the above primitive yet useful variety. Sometimes decisions partially interact with other decisions—variables are only partly influenced by one decision and are subject to further control by a later decision. In dynamic decision-making, a set of variables may be influenced by a decision but the possibility of their further *controlled* variation by later decisions is not ruled out. The simplest dynamic decision-making case which was encountered in this analysis was that in which the output which is planned for t in $t - n$ affects the cost of output in t but does not determine the output of t exactly.[4] The divergence of the actual output of t from the planned output depends upon the price which is eventually found to prevail for the product in t. In this case, only two decisions are related; each planned output decision for the output of n periods later interacts with the actual output decision of n periods later. We imagine that each planned output decision can be placed in a sequence, its order

[3] J. R. Hicks, *op. cit.*, Appendix to Ch. xv, Ch. xv.
[4] See Ch. vii.

depending on the last time point at which it can be made and suppose that each is delayed until this time point and that the delay involves no extra cost. Hence, *each chain* of two interdependent decisions can be treated independently.

Production relationships can involve dynamic decision-making models of varying degrees of complexity. Very long chains of interdependent decisions may arise or, as in the case just mentioned, short broken chains. But all have the characteristic that probable learning or changes of information are likely to influence some decisions because of their interdependence with other decisions which depend upon this learning or change of information. As the work of Bellman[5] and others indicate, some of these optimization problems are extremely complicated, but not all are beyond systematic analysis.

Examining Hicks' contribution in *Value and Capital* upon the (dynamic) production plan of the firm,[6] it is found that his formulation determines rigidly the optimal production values of the firm for an interval of N periods ahead, discount factors being taken into account. If the horizon remains fixed and if no relevant information change occurs prior to each possible decision, the Hicksian production values remain optimal throughout the time span, provided that the firm wishes to maximize its capitalized value of surpluses. However, these values need not remain optimal if information changes over time and if institutional and technical factors do not completely rule out the possibility of variations to take advantage of changes in the state of information.

For example, where $X_t, t = 1, \ldots, N$, represents a vector of commodity values at time period t, let $[X^*_1, X^*_2, \ldots, X^*_N]$ represent the optimal production solution for a firm, supposing that the Hicksian dynamic assumptions are applicable. But if we suppose that each of the X_t values can be determined independently and that each X_t value can be decided in $t - 1$

[5] R. E. Bellman and S. E. Dreyfus, *Applied Dynamic Programming*, Princeton University Press, Princeton, 1962.

[6] J. R. Hicks, *op. cit.*, Ch. xv and Appendix to it.

or before without loss to the firm, then, in general, one expects that actual and optimal production will diverge from the vector $[X^*_1, X^*_2, \ldots, X^*_N]$. If the firm is placed at period t_0, the optimal value of X_1 will remain unchanged at X^*_1, but later values may diverge from the previous production vector if changes of information cause the Hicksian anticipated price values to change over time. If the firm is placed at t_0, X_1 must be rigidly determined, but the choice of later production values remains a function or bears some relationship to future information and is not rigidly determined at t_0. Production choices beyond t_1 are contingent on changes of information or learning.

The previous assumptions about interdependence of decisions are to some extent particular. Production values at different time points may be interconnected but not inflexibly so. Extending the above example, assume that each X_t value is to be decided inflexibly one period in advance of its realization but that the X_t values are interconnected; e.g., the possible variation of X_t might depend upon the value of X_{t-1}. If learning is of importance, this interconnection further complicates choice. If the firm is situated at t_0, X^*_1 need no longer be the firm's optimal choice of X_1, for the optimal value of X_1 needs to be chosen in the light of its interconnection with other variables and their probable values, taking into account probable learning or changes of information over time. In these circumstances, the optimal strategy for a long period rarely consists of point values for production but may consist of rules for determining future values as a function of learning or information.

Now, the discounted price values which are used in the Hicksian objective function are assumed by Hicks to be adjusted so as to allow for risk or uncertainty. They are equal to "the most probable price ± an allowance for the uncertainty of the expectation, that is to say, an allowance for risk."[7] This, as Hicks points out, is not an entirely satisfactory method of

[7] J. R. Hicks, *op. cit.*, p. 126.

dealing with risk. It also gives us no information about the values of the appropriate allowance.

The approach does not bring out some of the problems which are associated with the determination of certainty equivalent prices. For example, if a firm wishes to maximize the *expected* value of some (objective) function which depends on the value of its controlled variables as well as on the value of its non-controlled variables, under what circumstances can it replace the values of the non-controlled variables in the function by their mean values and, by maximizing the resultant function, obtain values for its controlled variables which maximize the expected value of its (objective) function? As an example, suppose that the firm is involved in static decision-making and that it aims to maximize the expected value of its profit $\pi(X, P)$, where X represents the vector of the firm's controlled variables, i.e., production combinations, and P is a vector of the values of its non-controlled variables, i.e., the prices of the commodities. If $E[P]$ represents the vector of the mean values of the components of the vector P, and if X^* is the value of X which gives $\underset{X}{\text{Max }} \pi(X, E[P])$, under what circumstances is it also the value of X which gives $\underset{X}{\text{Max }} E[\pi(X, P)]$? If, as in the pure competition case, the profit function is *linear* in the price values, and if the only restriction of this function is due to restrictions imposed upon the controlled variables, then certainty equivalence exists. Theil and others have also shown that if the preference function happens to be quadratic in the non-controlled variables, then, for the static decision-making case, certainty equivalence occurs.[8] By substituting the mean values of the non-controlled variables for their actual values into the preference function and maximizing the resultant expression, one obtains values for the controlled variables which maximize the expected value of the preference function. In this quadratic case, if $U(X, P)$ represents the preference function, $E[U(X, P)]$ and

[8] H. Theil, *op. cit.*, pp. 414–424.

$U(X, E[P])$ differ by a constant, and hence the X value which maximizes one expression also maximizes the other. But for some forms of $U(X, P)$, the X value which maximizes $E[U(X, P)]$ is not the same as that which maximizes $U(X, E[P])$.[9]

If dynamic decision-making is possible, the expected profit maximization strategy becomes more complicated. In such cases, one decision may affect another, and the dependent decisions may be subject to variation which depends on learning. For some quadratic cases, such as the one considered in the analysis, *first-period* certainty equivalence exists. But there are some relationships for which even first-period certainty equivalence does not exist in Theil's sense.[10] Again, over long intervals of time, if learning is of importance the output strategies which maximize expected profit do not generally consist of point values but are some function of information. Not only is the expected profit maximization strategy subject to influence by the possibility of learning, but so also are the minimax and other strategies for choice under uncertainty.

Although certainty equivalence in Theil's sense does not always exist, and although optimal choices of production cannot always be stated in advance as point values, it does not thereby follow that no form of maximum equivalence exists. If production in the dynamic case satisfies conditions similar to those outlined in Chapters III and IV, e.g., the convexity conditions, then similar maximum equivalence theorems hold. For example, if production is at a boundary point which is *strictly* convex in the set of production possibilities, then at least one set of shadow prices yields the production combinations at this point if they are substituted into the profit function and the resultant function is maximized subject to the production possibility set. The possible application of the maximum equivalence theorems are the same as previously outlined— it is possible to discover the appropriate shadow prices in

[9] For some examples, see H. Theil, *op. cit.*, p. 418–423.
[10] Cf. Theil, *op. cit.*, pp. 505–522.

some problems, and they enable us to obtain further theorems which encompass the effects of diverse behavior; e.g., by using them, the results of Chapter IX can be extended to a longer time interval. Yet, if learning is of importance over time, it will be generally impossible to give for a long time interval the optimal or actual production values *in advance* as point values, and so also will it generally be impossible to set up in advance a maximum equivalence problem with point shadow price values.

Nothing has been postulated in the analysis about the ways in which images of possibilities form and change over time, although several economists have suggested some simple models of image formation.[11] For many of the theorems which were considered, a theory of image formation was found to be inessential. They are, however, of importance for some problems which are not considered, e.g., for the paths which output values will take over time.

The previous notes have indicated a few of the problems which one encounters in devising theories of optimal production behavior which apply to both uncertain and dynamic conditions. They have also set the analysis into a wider context. But some difficulties have not been considered; account has not been taken of the cost of the decision process itself and the optimality, therefore, of "imperfect" decisions.[12] Taking into account the costs of deciding on optimal decision processes and obvious rational limits on the process of deciding about decision processes, there would seem to be many circumstances in which optimal or rational behavior exhibits *random* variation. Frequently, rational behavior may not be *exactly* determinate in advance. Indeed, in practice, rational (reasonable) behavior

[11] For a brief survey of theories about the formation of price expectations, see E. S. Mills, *Price, Output, and Inventory Policy*, John Wiley and Sons, New York, 1962, Ch. 3, "The Analysis of Expectations."

[12] Cf. E. S. Mills, *op. cit.*, Ch. 2, and especially W. J. Baumol and R. E. Quandt, "Rules of Thumb and Optimally Imperfect Decisions," *American Economic Review*, vol. 54 (1964), pp. 23–46. Also, T. C. Koopmans, *Three Essays on the State of the Economic Science*, McGraw–Hill, New York, 1957, pp. 160–165.

may nearly always involve a random element because of limitations imposed by the costs of calculation.

C. Miscellaneous Matters

A firm's price uncertainty may arise from several sources: from uncertainty of industry demand, from technological uncertainty, from uncertainty about the actions of other firms in the industry, and from other sources such as ignorance about the market mechanism itself. While any of these factors can give rise to price uncertainty, in this analysis, technological uncertainty has been excluded. Scope exists for further developing the analysis to take technological uncertainty into account.[13]

The concept of equilibrium has played an unimportant role in the analysis. This may have helped rather than hindered us in obtaining useful theorems. It is hard to avoid the conclusion that the concept of equilibrium has played considerable havoc with economic theory. The concept's present mystical aura seems to act as a psychological barrier diverting attention from a thorough study of those *processes* or mechanisms of resource allocation which operate in an uncertain and changing world, a world in which knowledge is ever changing. Because of the preoccupation in economics with formal equilibrium conditions, several processes of resource allocation have not been carefully analyzed, and some allocation theories, especially general equilibrium ones, have assumed an air of unreality and irrelevance. For example, the role of information and imperfections or frictions in resource allocation processes has not been adequately analyzed.[14]

[13] Much attention has already been given to technological uncertainty in economic theory. For example, Tintner has explored the subject. See G. Tintner, "A Pure Theory of Production under Technological Risk and Uncertainty," *Econometrica*, vol. 9 (1941), pp. 305–312.

[14] This objection is by no means new. See, for example, O. Morgenstern, "Perfect Foresight and Economic Equilibrium," *Zeitschrift für Nationalökonomie*, vol. 5 (1935), for a study of some of the difficulties which knowledge creates for the concept of equilibrium. See also G. B. Richardson, "Equilibrium, Expectations and Information," *Economic Journal*, vol. 69 (1959), pp. 223–227.

Let us briefly mention some points on the last subject which require analytical clarification. Without wishing to be pedantic, let us note that it is not always the case, as is sometimes erroneously suggested, that reduced frictions (time lags, obstructions, or immobilities) in a market increase the probability that an equilibrium will be reached, more closely approximated, or attained or approximated more quickly. This is so because of the barriers to equilibrium which are imposed by imperfections in knowledge, especially those difficulties which arise in learning about the actions of others in the market. Knowledge about others' actions may not be increased by an increase in the mobility of resources, and one cannot conclude, *a priori*, that the more mobile resources are the more likely is it that a market will attain equilibrium. The existence of friction in an economic system may result in learning and response patterns which ensure a more probable convergence to equilibrium. Because of difficulties entailed in each firm's learning about the proposed actions of all other firms in a market, "superior" allocative systems may be ones which entail some types of imperfection, e.g., lags and immobilities in factor movements; neither extreme imperfection nor extreme mobility being ideal. Our understanding of processes of resource allocation might be greatly improved by a detailed analysis of this and similar matters. Recent developments in cybernetics or abstract control processes[15] might prove to be fruitful guides in such a study.

Many of the relationships which are suggested in this analysis can be subjected to empirical investigation. For example, one might investigate the influence of actual forward price schemes on output, or one might consider whether there is any empirical evidence in favor of the suggestion in Chapter V that in reaction to increased price uncertainty firms tend to reduce their output response to actual price changes. At a

[15] See R. Bellman, *Adaptive Control Processes: A Guided Tour*, Princeton University Press, Princeton, 1961; N. Wiener, *Cybernetics*, John Wiley and Sons, New York, 1948. The interested reader will find many references to the literature in Bellman's book.

more pedestrian level, one may wish to measure the extent of divergencies among firms in their price "anticipations" or shadow prices and, in view of these, use the analysis to draw quantitative conclusions. One can, of course, extend the list further. It is also evident that the analysis has implications for the derivation of statistical supply curves—price uncertainty sometimes results in their systematic bias away from the certainty supply curve, and "the influences" are readily isolated.

D. Conclusions of the Analysis

It would be superfluous to repeat here those conclusions which were outlined for each chapter. But the general path of development might be indicated again. The analysis began by considering abstract theories of behavior and decision-making under uncertainty, and went on to apply some of these to the static production decisions of a firm operating under price uncertainty. Then, it dealt with the influence of price uncertainty and instability upon the firm's average profit and choice of (production) techniques, first employing a static decision-making assumption and then a dynamic decision-making one. Attention next shifted to the influence of price uncertainty and instability upon industry's profit. The analysis then proceeded beyond this to consider the effect of price uncertainty upon the economy's level of aggregate production and consumption and the scope which may exist for forward price schemes to increase the economy's production and consumption by reducing price uncertainty. Finally, this chapter has suggested some possible extensions of the analysis.

"The maximum equivalence principle" has been of considerable value in the analysis, since it has enabled us to obtain general theorems in circumstances where the behavior of economic agents is diverse. This I felt to be important, since I am skeptical about the possibility of encompassing all economic behavior exactly in a single simple theory. Keynes implies something similar when he suggests "that it is our innate urge to activity which makes the wheels go round, our rational selves choosing between the alternatives as best we are able, calculating where we can, but often falling back for our motive on whim or sentiment or chance."[16] It is not that economic behavior shows no regularity but that it does not exhibit such perfect uniformity as is sometimes supposed. However, as the analysis has indicated, even diverse behavior has regular and discoverable consequences.

To conclude: There can be no doubt that man's imperfect knowledge has important consequences for his behavior. By continuing to study the impact of knowledge, learning, and uncertainty upon behavior, we can hope to obtain a better understanding of the economic and social universe. It seems possible that many of the fundamental influences of imperfect knowledge on social and economic life are, as yet, only dimly perceived and await serious analysis.

[16] J. M. Keynes, *The General Theory of Employment, Interest and Money,* Macmillan, London, 1936, p. 163.

APPENDIX I

A Brief Note on the Introduction
of Inventories into the Analysis

A. Introduction

Inventories were excluded from the analysis in order to simplify it. The purpose of this appendix is to show some of the ways in which they can be introduced. Yet it is not intended to begin an extensive study of optimal inventory policies[1] or to rework the analysis. The few observations which are to be made will be directed first toward the introduction of inventories into static decision-making models. Then, inventories will be considered in a dynamic decision-making context.

B. Inventories in Static Decision-Making Models

As previously, let us treat time as a discrete variable. Also, let us assume that the firm operates under pure competition and produces one product. Then, a simple but trivial introduction of inventories is possible if it is supposed that all the output (or purchases) of any period must be stored for a given length of time and cannot be stored any longer. For example, take the case which was considered in Chapter V. Suppose that at $t - n$, $n \geq 1$, that the firm "must" decide inflexibly on its output (or, where appropriate, purchases) of $t - \theta$, $1 \leq \theta \leq n$, and that this quantity must be stored until t when it is always sold. Our previous static decision-making results then apply *mutatis mutandis*, if each such decision is independent of every other. In the reformulation, the costs of storage[2] need only be added to the costs of production.

---

[1] For extensive studies, which do take uncertainty into account, see K. J. Arrow, S. Karlin, and H. Scarf, *Studies in the Mathematical Theory of Inventory and Production*, Stanford University Press, Stanford 1958; G. Hadley and T. M. Whitin, *Analysis of Inventory Systems*, Prentice-Hall, Englewood Cliffs, 1963.

Similarly, a simple extension of the dynamic decision-making model of Chapter VII is possible. For instance, imagine that while at $t - n$, $n \geq 2$, a decision is always made upon the output of $t - \theta$, $1 \leq \theta \leq n$, the firm can diverge from this output during $t - \theta$ at a cost, the final output of $t - \theta$ being stored until t when it is sold. The results of Chapter VII can then be extended in a straightforward way. However, these cases introduce inventories in a trivial fashion, for they assume that, subject to a constant lag, sales equal previous output.

Let us consider a case in which this is not assumed. Suppose that the firm decides inflexibly at $t - n$, $n \geq 1$, on its output and sales for period t. Also assume that the stored production of any period is held inflexibly for Λ periods, $\Lambda \geq 1$, and is then sold. Hence, if a firm is placed at $t - n$, it is faced with a decision on its output of t and on the quantity of this to store until $t + \Lambda$ for sale then. If each of these decisions is independent of every other, it is not difficult to determine the firm's optimal production level for period t and the optimal quantity of production to store. It may be helpful to outline an optimal solution first of all for a case in which the firm knows its prices and wishes to maximize its profit.

Let p_t represent the price of the firm's product for period t, $C_t(x_t)$ represent its total cost of producing an output of x_t in period t, $p_{t+\Lambda}$ indicate the price of the product in period $t + \Lambda$, and $h_t(I_t)$ represent the cost of storing a level I_t of the product from period t to period $t + \Lambda$. Assume that $C_t(x_t)$ and $h_t(I_t)$ are differentiable functions and that $C_t(x_t)$ and $C_t(x_t) + h_t(x_t)$ are strictly convex and increasing functions of their arguments. Then, the optimal value of x_t can be determined by the following procedure.[3] Let

$$p_t = C'_t(x_t) \qquad \text{A.1}$$

---

[2] The cost of storage of any period's output is assumed to depend *only* on the stored quantity of that period's output. If it depends on accumulated inventories, a dynamic decision-making problem can arise.

[3] Fixed costs are ignored in the following argument. It is possible that some additional fixed cost may be incurred if one decides to hold some of the production of a period.

for

$$x_t = \bar{x}_t,$$

and let

$$p_{t+\Lambda} = C'_t(x_t) + h'_t(x_t) \qquad\qquad \text{A.2}$$

for

$$x_t = \tilde{x}_t.$$

Then, if $\tilde{x}_t \geq \bar{x}_t$, the optimal value of x_t, x^*_t, equals $\tilde{x}_t$. If $\tilde{x}_t < \bar{x}_t$, $x^*_t = \bar{x}_t$. It is optimal to produce an output during t up to *at least* that level at which the marginal costs of its production equal the marginal revenue from its sale in period t. Also, it is optimal to produce an output during t up to *at least* that level at which the marginal costs of its production plus the marginal costs of its storage equals the marginal revenue from its sale in period $t + \Lambda$. It is optimal to produce the larger of these two quantities. This determines only the optimal value of x_t and not the optimal value of I_t. Let us now determine this.

In determining the optimal value of I_t, account must be taken of inequality restrictions upon its possible value. For example, if $x_t = x^*_t$, I_t is restricted to the range $0 \leq I_t \leq x^*_t$. If $p_{t+\Lambda} \leq p_t$, the optimal value of I_t will be zero, but if $p_{t+\Lambda} > p_t$, the optimal value may be positive. If $p_{t+\Lambda} > p_t$, the optimal value of I_t, I^*_t, can be determined by the following procedure if the holding of inventories does not involve an additional fixed cost and if $h'_t(I_t)$ is a monotonically increasing function. Let

$$p_{t-\Lambda} - p_t = h'_t(I_t) \qquad\qquad \text{A.3}$$

for $I_t = \tilde{I}_t$.

Then, if $0 \leq \tilde{I}_t \leq x^*_t$, $I^*_t = \tilde{I}_t$. If $\tilde{I}_t > x^*_t$, $I^*_t = x^*_t$. Now, consider the case in which marginal costs are constant. In this case, if $h'_t(I_t) = a$ and if $a < p_{t-\Lambda} - p_t$, $I^*_t = x^*_t$, and, if the inequality is reversed, $I^*_t = 0$. Again, if $h'_t(I_t)$ is a monotonically decreasing function, if no additional fixed costs are involved in carrying inventories, and if $p_{t-\Lambda} - p_t > h'_t(0)$, $I^*_t = x^*_t$. From these results on optimal output and inventory values, it is, of course, easy to determine the optimal level of sales.

Price uncertainty can be introduced into this model without difficulty, for, if only the prices of the product are uncertain, the firm's objective function is linear in its non-controlled variables. If the firm wishes to maximize its expected profit and knows its costs, then its optimal output and inventory values can be determined by substituting expected price values for prices in the above argument and reinterpreting accordingly. If the firm adopts a maximin gain approach to uncertainty, its optimal inventory and output values can be found by substituting the lowest "possible" values of p_t and $p_{t+\Lambda}$ into the above argument. For a maximax approach, the highest possible price values should be substituted into the above argument. If the range of possible $p_{t+\Lambda}$ values tends to exceed that for the possible p_t values, there is a tendency for inventories to be lowest for the maximin gain criterion, higher for the expected profit criterion, and highest for the maximax. The discussion of Chapter VIII can also be easily recast in terms of this model.

More complicated static decision-making models which incorporate inventories are available.[4] But it seems that dynamic decision-making models are more appropriate for cases which involve inventories and extend over a long time period. Over "long" periods of time, inflexible point plans are rarely optimal because learning takes place and can often be used to advantage.

C. Inventories in Dynamic Decision-Making Models

It is a characteristic of dynamic decision-making that, while some decisions influence others, they do not determine them exactly. In dynamic decision-making, some future choices are random, their probability distribution being determined by other choices and the possibilities for learning. Generally, in dynamic decision-making optimal strategies

[4] See, for example, E. S. Mills, *Price, Output, and Inventory Policy*, John Wiley, New York, 1962, Ch. 4; Arrow *et al.*, *op. cit.*

cannot be expressed as point values but are functions of learning or of changes of knowledge. Earlier decisions need to be
chosen in the light of their probable influence upon later ones,
and this can give rise to very complicated decision problems.

Production decisions which involve inventories are frequently dynamic decision-making ones. If the costs of storage
of inventories depends on their *accumulated* quantities and if
learning takes place about future prices, the choices of inventory levels at different times are interdependent and the later
choices will vary depending on learning. Hence, dynamic
decision-making is involved.[5] But to give a less complicated
example, suppose that at $t - n$ a decision must be reached on
the output of t and imagine that any of the production of t
which is not sold in t is held until $t + \Lambda$ when it is sold. Also,
assume that the cost of holding the production of t depends
only on the quantity of it held I_t and that the firm has a last
choice on I_t in t. Suppose that in $t - n$ the firm knows p_t but
not $p_{t+\Lambda}$. Then, its sales in t will be varied depending upon
what it then "knows about" $p_{t+\Lambda}$ and the costs of varying from
any original plan on I_t. These possibilities need to be taken
into account in reaching an optimal decision in $t - n$ on
production. If allowing for these variations, it is possible to
express the objective function in a suitable quadratic form, it is
possible to obtain optimal first-period values by using the
certainty equivalence principle.[6]

But this is a special case. In the main, dynamic decision-
making problems are difficult to solve analytically, and the
difficulties are increased by the presence of inequalities such as
those introduced by inventories. Computational techniques
such as dynamic programming have evolved to solve some of
the problems,[7] and they have sometimes been approximated

[5] For further discussions of inventories in dynamic decision-making
models, see Mills, *op. cit.*, Chs. 6 and 7 or the references listed under
footnote 1.

[6] H. Theil, *Economic Forecasts and Policy*, 2nd revised edn., North-
Holland Publishing Company, Amsterdam, 1961, Ch. 8.

[7] R. E. Bellman and S. E. Dreyfus, *Applied Dynamic Programming*,
Princeton University Press, Princeton, 1962.

by one-stage problems.[8] Where these "one-stage" approximations only amount to a replacement of the extensive form of
the decision by its normal form, they really ignore many difficulties, since great effort and cost may be involved in deriving
the normal form; indeed, the whole process *may* involve as
much effort as direct enumeration.

Again, costs of calculation can have an important bearing
upon optimal decision processes.[9] They can make it optimal
to approximate dynamic decision-making problems by
simpler ones and act upon the basis of these. Clearly, such
approximation may give rise to apparent randomness of
behavior. From both normative and descriptive points of
view, studies of optimally imperfect decisions promise to be
rewarding. Some existing normative theories of behavior
may correspond poorly with observed behavior, and they can
be sub-optimal in a wider context in which some weight is
given to the cost of a decision. But a study of this matter must
rest with the future.

D. Conclusion

The introduction of inventories brings to the fore many of
the great problems which time raises for economic choice.
It emphasizes the interdependence of decisions in time and
indicates some of the important influences upon choice which
occur because we live both in a world of uncertainty and in a
world of changing knowledge. It also strengthens our conviction that calculation costs have an important impact upon
the optimality of decisions and actual choices.

[8] See Arrow, *et al.*, *op. cit.*
[9] Cf. Mills, *op. cit.*

BIBLIOGRAPHY

Only those works which are mentioned in the analysis are included in this bibliography.

Allen, R. G. D., *Mathematical Analysis for Economists*, Macmillan, London, 1960.

Arrow, K. J., *Aspects of the Theory of Risk-Bearing*, Yrjö Jahnsson Lectures, The Academic Bookstore, Helsinki, 1965.

Arrow, K. J., S. Karlin, and H. Scarf, *Studies in the Mathematical Theory of Inventory and Production*, Stanford University Press, Stanford, 1958.

Barone, E., "The Ministry of Production in the Collectivist State," pp. 245–290 in *Collectivist Economic Planning*, F. A. von Hayek, ed., George Routledge and Sons, London, 1935.

Baumol, W. J., *Economic Dynamics*, 2nd edn., The Macmillan Company, New York, 1959.

Baumol, W. J., and R. E. Quandt, "Rules of Thumb and Optimally Imperfect Decisions," *American Economic Review*, vol. 54 (1964), pp. 23–46.

Bayes, Thomas, "An Essay Towards Solving a Problem in the Doctrine of Chances," reprinted in *Biometrika*, vol. 45 (1958), parts 3 and 4, pp. 296–315.

Bellman, R., *Adaptive Control Processes: A Guided Tour*, Princeton University Press, Princeton, 1961.

Bellman, R. E., and S. E. Dreyfus, *Applied Dynamic Programming*, Princeton University Press, Princeton, 1962.

Bernoulli, Daniel, "Specimen theoriae novae de mensura sortis," *Comentari academiae scientarum imperialis Petropolitanae*, vol. 5 (1738). Translated by Dr Louise Sommer as "Exposition of a New Theory on the Measurement of Risk," *Econometrica*, vol. 12 (1954), pp. 23–36.

Boulding, K. E., *The Image*, The University of Michigan Press, Ann Arbor, 1956.

——, *Conflict and Defense*, Harper and Brothers, New York, 1962.

Carnap, R., *Logical Foundations of Probability*, The University of Chicago Press, Chicago, 1950.

Carter, C. F., G. P. Meredith, and G. L. S. Shackle, eds., *Uncertainty and Business Decisions*, The University Press, Liverpool, 1954.

Chernoff, H., "Rational Selection of Decision Functions," *Econometrica*, vol. 22 (1954), pp. 442–443.

Courant, R., *Differential and Integral Calculus*, Vol. I, Interscience Publishers, New York, 1937.

Dewey, J., *The Quest for Certainty*, G. P. Putnam's Sons, New York, 1960.

Domar, E., and R. Musgrave, "Proportional Income Taxation and Risk-Taking," *Quarterly Journal of Economics*, vol. 58 (1944), pp. 388–422.

Dreyfus, S. E., see under Bellman, R. E.

Fellner, W., *Probability and Profit*, Richard D. Irwin, Homewood, Ill., 1965.

de Finetti, B., "La prévision: ses lois logiques, ses sources subjectives," *Annales de l'Institut Henri Poincairé*, vol. 7 (1937), pp. 1–68.

Hadley, G., and T. M. Whitin, *Analysis of Inventory Systems*, Prentice-Hall, Englewood Cliffs, 1963.

Hardy, G. H., J. E. Littlewood, and G. Polya, *Inequalities*, Cambridge University Press, Cambridge, 1934.

Hart, A. G., "Risk, Uncertainty, and the Unprofitability of Compounding Probabilities," pp. 110–118 in *Studies in Mathematical Economics and Econometrics*, O. Lange, F. McIntyre, and F. Yntema, eds., The University of Chicago Press, Chicago, 1942.

Henderson, J. M., and R. E. Quandt, *Microeconomic Theory*, McGraw-Hill Book Company, New York, 1958.

Hicks, J. R., *Value and Capital*, 2nd edn., The Clarendon Press, Oxford, 1946.

Hurwicz, L., "Optimality Criteria for Decision Making under Ignorance," Cowles Commission Discussion Paper, No. 370, 1950. Mimeographed.

Jeffreys, H., *Theory of Probability*, 2nd edn., The Clarendon Press, Oxford, 1948.

Johnson, D. G., *Forward Prices for Agriculture*, The University of Chicago Press, Chicago, 1947.

Karlin, S., "Matrix Games, Programming and Mathematical Economics," *Mathematical Methods and Theory of Games, Programming and Economics*, Vol. I, Addison-Wesley Publishing Company, Reading, 1959.

——, see under Arrow, K. J.

Keynes, J. M., *A Treatise on Probability*, Macmillan, London, 1921.

Keynes, J. M., *The General Theory of Employment, Interest and Money*, Macmillan, London, 1936.

Khinchin, A. I., *Mathematical Foundations of Information Theory*, Dover Publications, New York, 1959.

Knight, F. H., *Risk, Uncertainty, and Profit*, Houghton Mifflin Company, New York, 1922.

Kolmogorov, A. N., *Foundations of the Theory of Probability*, Chelsea Publishing Company, New York, 1950.

Koopmans, T. C., *Three Essays on the State of Economic Science*, McGraw-Hill, New York, 1957.

Lange, O., "On the Economic Theory of Socialism," pp. 55–142 in *On the Economic Theory of Socialism*, B. Lippincott, ed., The University of Minnesota Press, Minneapolis, 1938.

Littlewood, J. E., see under Hardy, G. H.

Luce, R. D., and H. Raiffa, *Games and Decisions*, John Wiley, New York, 1957.

Markowitz, H. M., *Portfolio Selection—Efficient Diversifications of Investments*, John Wiley, New York, 1959.

Marschak, J., "Utilities and Probabilities in Human Choice," an abstract in *Report of Third Annual Research Conference on Economics and Statistics*, Colorado Springs, 1937.

——, "Money and the Theory of Assets," *Econometrica*, vol. 6 (1938), pp. 311–325.

——, "Probability in the Social Sciences," pp. 166–215 in *Mathematical Thinking in the Social Sciences*, P. L. Lazarsfeld, ed., The Free Press, Glencoe, Ill., 1954.

Marschak, T., and R. Nelson, "Flexibility, Uncertainty and Economic Theory," *Metroeconomica*, vol. 14 (1962), pp. 42–58.

Mills, Edwin S., *Price, Output, and Inventory Policy*, John Wiley, New York, 1962.

Milnor, J., "Games Against Nature," pp. 49–59 in *Decision Processes*, R. M. Thrall, C. H. Coombs, and R. L. Davis, eds., John Wiley, New York, 1954.

von Mises, L., "Economic Calculation in the Socialist Commonwealth," pp. 87–130 in *Collectivist Economic Planning*, F. A. von Hayek, ed., George Routledge and Sons, London, 1935.

von Mises, R., *Probability, Statistics and Truth*, 2nd edn., George Allen and Unwin, London, 1957.

Morgenstern, O., "Perfect Foresight and Economic Equilibrium," *Zeitschrift für Nationalökonomie*, Vol. 5 (1935).

——, see under von Neumann, J.

Musgrave, R., see under Domar, E.

Nelson, R. R., "Uncertainty Prediction and Competitive Equilibrium," *The Quarterly Journal of Economics*, vol. 75 (1961), pp. 41–62.

——, see under Marschak, T.

von Neumann, J., and O. Morgenstern, *Theory of Games and Economic Behavior*, Princeton University Press, Princeton, 1st edn., 1944; 3rd edn., 1953.

Oi, W. Y., "The Desirability of Price Instability under Perfect Competition," *Econometrica*, vol. 29 (1961), pp. 58–64.

——, "Rejoinder," *Econometrica*, vol. 31 (1963), p. 248.

Passmore, J., *One Hundred Years of Philosophy*, G. Duckworth, London, 1957.

Pearce, I. F., *A Contribution to Demand Analysis*, The Clarendon Press, Oxford, 1964.

Polya, G., see under Hardy, G. H.

Quandt, R. E., see under Baumol, W. J. and under Henderson, J. M.

Radner, R., "Mathematical Specifications of Goals for Decision Problems," Ch. 11 in *Human Judgments and Optimality*, M. W. Shelly and G. L. Bryan, eds., John Wiley, New York, 1964.

Raiffa, H., see under Luce, R. D.

Ramsey, F. P., "Truth and Probability" (1926), essay VII in *The Foundations of Mathematics and Other Logical Essays*, R. Braithwaite, ed., Routledge and Kegan Paul, London, 1931.

Reichenbach, H., *The Theory of Probability*, University of California Press, Berkeley, 1949.

Richardson, G. B., "Equilibrium, Expectations and Information," *Economic Journal*, vol. 69 (1959), pp. 223–227.

Roy, A. D., "Safety First and the Holding of Assets," *Econometrica*, vol. 20 (1952), pp. 431–449.

Russell, B., "Can Men Be Rational?" Ch. 4 in *Sceptical Essays*, Unwin Books, London, 1960.

Samuelson, P. A., *Foundations of Economic Analysis*, Harvard University Press, Cambridge, 1947.

Savage, L. J., "The Theory of Statistical Decision," *Journal of the American Statistical Association*, vol. 46 (1951), 55–67.

——, *The Foundations of Statistics*, John Wiley, New York, 1954.

Scarf, H., see under Arrow, K. J.

Shackle, G. L. S., *Expectation in Economics*, The University Press, Cambridge, 1949.

——, *Uncertainty in Economics*, The University Press, Cambridge, 1955.

——, *Time in Economics*, North-Holland Publishing Company, Amsterdam, 1958.

Simon, H. A., "A Behavioral Model of Rational Choice," *Quarterly Journal of Economics*, vol. 79, 1955, pp. 99–118.

——, "Dynamic Programming under Uncertainty with a Quadratic Criterion Function," *Econometrica*, vol. 24 (1956), pp. 74–81.

——, *Models of Man*, John Wiley, New York, 1957.

Soper, C. S., and L. Webb, "Tisdell on Uncertainty and Pareto Optimality," *Economic Record*, vol. 40 (1964), pp. 581–590.

Stigler, G. J., "Production and Distribution in the Short Run," *Journal of Political Economy*, vol. 47 (1939), pp. 305–328.

Taylor, F. M., "The Guidance of Production in a Socialist State," pp. 41–54 in *On the Economic Theory of Socialism*, B. Lippincott, ed., The University of Minnesota Press, Minneapolis, 1938.

Theil, H., "Econometric Models and Welfare Maximization," *Weltwirtschaftliches Archiv*, vol. 72 (1954), pp. 60–83.

——, "A Note on Certainty Equivalence in Dynamic Planning," *Econometrica*, vol. 25 (1957), pp. 346–349.

——, *Economic Forecasts and Policy*, 2nd revised edn., North-Holland Publishing Company, 1961.

——, "Some Reflections on Static Programming under Uncertainty," *Weltwirtschaftliches Archiv*, vol. 87 (1961), pp. 124–138.

Tintner, G., "A Pure Theory of Production under Technological Risk and Uncertainty," *Econometrica*, vol. 9 (1941), pp. 305–312.

——, "A Contribution to the Nonstatic Theory of Production," pp. 92–109 in *Studies in Mathematical Economics and Econometrics*, O. Lange, F. McIntyre and T. O. Yntema, eds., University of Chicago Press, Chicago, 1942.

——, "Foundations of Probability and Statistical Inference," *Journal of the Royal Statistical Society*, Vol. 112, Part III (1949), pp. 251–279.

Tisdell, C., "Decision Making and the Probability of Loss," *Australian Economic Papers*, vol. 1 (1962), pp. 109–118.

——, "Uncertainty and Pareto Optimality," *Economic Record*, vol. 39 (1963), pp. 405–412.

——, "A Rejoinder," *Economic Record*, vol. 40 (1964), pp. 590–596.

——, "Some Bounds upon the Pareto Optimality of Group Behavior," *Kyklos*, vol. 19 (1966), pp. 81–105.

Venn, J., *Logic of Chance*, 2nd edn., Macmillan, London, 1876.

Venttsel', E. S., *An Introduction to the Theory of Games*, D. C. Heath and Co., Boston, 1963.

Wald, A., *Statistical Decision Functions*, John Wiley, New York, 1950.

Weatherburn, C. E., *A First Course in Mathematical Statistics*, The University Press, Cambridge, 1961.

Webb, L., see under Soper, C. S.

Whitin, T. M., see under Hadley, G.

Wiener, N., *Cybernetics*, John Wiley, New York, 1948.

Index

Allen, R. G. D., 12
anticipated profit criterion, 47
Arrow, K. J., 26, 184, 189

Barone, E., 167
Baumol, W. J., 11, 17, 106–109, 179
Bayes, T., 23
Bayes criterion, 23, 35; *applied* to one-product firm's output 49, 78, 79; to multi-commodity case, 65; to inventories, 187. *See also* expected gain criterion
behavior, general theories of, 4, 6. *See also* rational behavior, consistent behavior
Bellman, R. E., 125, 175, 181, 188
Bernoulli, D., 24, 25
Boulding, K. E., 14, 15, 18
bounded rationality, 16, 36–38, 179

Carnap, R., 20
Carter, C., 29
central planning, 167–69
certainty equivalence, 124, 126, 177–78
commutativity, 61, 62
complementarity, 74
consistent behavior, 7; a theory 39, 40; related to rational behavior, 40
convex sets, some relevant maximization theorems, 50–52, 68–70
convexity, significance for average profit, 105
Courant, R., 76
cybernetics, 181

decision criteria, consistency with rational behavior, 22, 23, 35, 36; outlined, 23–34; their differing effects on production, 77–80
decision set of prices, 42, 46, 54; effect of its variation on

production, 75–77; related to actual prices, 81
determinism, 5
Dewey, J., 3
Domar, E., 28
dominance, 57
Dreyfus, S. E., 125, 175, 189
dynamic decision-making, 9, 10, 123–37, 174–79
dynamic programming, 125, 188

entropy formula, 92
equilibrium, 168, 180
errors of prediction, 5
expected gain criterion, 23, 24. *See also* Bayes criterion
expected utility rule, 24–27
expected value, of a polynomial function, 12, 26, 27; of a quadratic function, 12, 13

Fellner, W., 21
Finetti, B. de, 20
flexibility, 11, 106–107
forward price schemes, 12, 155–67, 170

general equilibrium, 12

Hadley, G., 184
Hardy, G. H., 105
Hart, A. G., 9, 11, 106, 172
Hayek, F. A. von, 167
Henderson, J. M., 166
Hicks, J. R., 9, 67, 68, 70, 74, 171 ff
Hurwicz, L., 33
Hurwicz criterion, outlined, 33; limitation, 34; *applied* to one-product firm's output, 48, 49, 65; to multi-commodity firm, 63, 64; related to maximax and minimax criteria, 48, 49

images, and rational behavior, 15; formation, 17

195

Milton Keynes UK
Ingram Content Group UK Ltd.
UKHW021821151223
434462UK00009B/709